Early Islam in Medina

Also Available from Bloomsbury

Metaphors of Death and Resurrection in the Qur'an, Abdulla Galadari
The Qur'an and Modern Arabic Literary Criticism, Mohammad Salama
Salvation and Hell in Classical Islamic Thought, Marco Demichelis

Early Islam in Medina

Mālik and His Muwaṭṭaʾ

Yasin Dutton

BLOOMSBURY ACADEMIC
LONDON • NEW YORK • OXFORD • NEW DELHI • SYDNEY

BLOOMSBURY ACADEMIC
Bloomsbury Publishing Plc
50 Bedford Square, London, WC1B 3DP, UK
1385 Broadway, New York, NY 10018, USA
29 Earlsfort Terrace, Dublin 2, Ireland

BLOOMSBURY, BLOOMSBURY ACADEMIC and the Diana logo are trademarks of Bloomsbury Publishing Plc

First published in Great Britain 2022
This paperback edition published 2023

Cover design: Tjasa Krivec
Cover image: Al-Masjid al-Nabawi - Medina, Saudi Arabia - Courtyard. Date: circa 1910s (© Chronicle / Alamy Stock Photo)

A catalogue record for this book is available from the British Library.

Library of Congress Control Number: 2021942924

ISBN: HB: 978-1-3502-6186-0
PB: 978-1-3502-6190-7
ePDF: 978-1-3502-6187-7
eBook: 978-1-3502-6188-4

Typeset by NewgenKnowledgeWorks Pvt. Ltd., Chennai, India

Contents

List of tables vi
A note on the text vii

Introduction 1
1 The man and his family 9
2 His teachers 15
3 The *Muwaṭṭaʾ* 39
4 The *ʿamal* of the people of Medina 63
5 Controversies, ancient and modern 79
Conclusion 117

Glossary 119
Notes 123
Bibliography 135
Index 141

Tables

1 Mālik's Main Teachers 16

2 Differences between the Transmissions in the Book of *Zakāt* 51

3 Differences between the Transmissions in the Book of Fasting 56

A note on the text

For the sake of brevity and in order not to overburden the text, I have aimed to minimize references where the material is commonly available in multiple sources and not subject to dispute. (This is especially the case with the more biographical material in Chapter 1.) I have, however, relied heavily on two works in particular which I do reference where appropriate within the text. These are Ibn ʿAbd al-Barr's *Kitāb al-Tamhīd* (especially in Chapter 2) and Qadi ʿIyāḍ's *Tartīb al-Madārik* (especially in Chapter 4). This is no accident. Both authors were giants in their field, and, as far as their knowledge is concerned, it would be decidedly perverse to try to reinvent the wheel. I have therefore accorded them a high degree of trust in what they have transmitted.

As is the practice in books relating to the early Islamic period, dates are given in both the traditional Hijrī dating (which is how they are found in the sources) and also in their equivalent Common Era form. However, although I have tried to exercise common sense when converting from one to the other, the mismatch between a year in the Hijrī lunar calendar and a year in the Common Era solar calendar means that an exact equivalent is not always identifiable; and where, for example, a number of options are given for a person's date of death in Hijrī terms, it has seemed too pedantic to give 'double' options for all possible dates in Common Era terms. It should therefore be remembered that, although I have aimed at accuracy in every instance, it may not have always been attained. In short, dates in general should be treated with a certain amount of caution.

Several key Arabic terms are used throughout the text in a transliterated form. These are explained at their first usage and also listed in the Glossary. Honorific titles such as 'Qadi' and 'Imam' have been Anglicized and used in front of names which are commonly referred to with those titles. Where there is uncertainty about the spelling or identification of a name, this is indicated by a question mark in brackets.

The reader should also be aware at the outset that this text is not a biography of Mālik, although it does contain significant biographical material about him.

Nor is it a history of the Mālikī school, or of any of the other schools, although it does contain significant reference to their historical development. In particular, it should be noted that the general purview is one of a pre-*madhhab* (school of law) time before the development of any distinction between 'Sunnī' and 'Shīʿī' schools of law.

All translations from classical Arabic texts are my own.

Introduction

This book follows on from two particular works of mine on the subject. In the first, *The Origins of Islamic Law: The Qur'an, the* Muwaṭṭaʾ *and Madinan* ʿAmal (1999), I aimed to provide a more nuanced understanding of the bases of Islamic law whereby the Qur'an is seen as the stimulus of a legal activity which is initially expressed through the non-textual sources of *sunna* ('normative practice', especially of the Prophet) and *ʿamal* ('practice', especially the Practice of the People of Medina), rather than the textual source of *ḥadīth* ('reports') as is usually assumed. These themes were continued in *Original Islam: Mālik and the* Madhhab *of Madina* (2007), where the aim was to negotiate medieval discussions of the same to a modern readership. In the present work, *Early Islam in Medina: Mālik and his* Muwaṭṭaʾ, we go beyond the first two, filling in certain gaps and expanding certain arguments, in order to arrive at a better understanding of the early period of Islam and its subsequent development.

One might ask, what is the importance of Mālik and his *Muwaṭṭaʾ*? An initial answer might be that Mālik is one of the founders – if we can accept that term – of one of the four, still existing, main Sunni schools of Islamic law – that of the Mālikīs. (The other three are the Ḥanafīs, the Shāfiʿīs, and the Ḥanbalīs, although historically there were others; there are of course other schools among the Shīʿa.) One might also say that Mālik's *Muwaṭṭaʾ* is effectively the first complete formulation of Islamic law – complete in the sense of providing some coverage of all the main topics. Or one might say that it is one of the earliest extensive collections of Prophetic *ḥadīth* and thus is significant in a textual history sense.

It is all these things, but in a sense its importance lies beyond all of these considerations. It presents what is possibly our earliest picture of a fully functioning Muslim society, not in its sociological sense – although there is some reference to that – but as a portrait of the prime legal parameters within which that society lived, that is, the parameters of Islam. Most importantly, it shows us an Islam that manifested primarily as action, rather than the written word.

The context of this book is the context of contemporary Euro-American scholarship on Islamic studies, particularly regarding the origins of Islamic law. For most of the twentieth century, the field seems to have been dominated by two figures, Ignaz Goldziher and Joseph Schacht. (It is significant that both Goldziher and Schacht were the authors of the articles on 'Fiḳh' (= *fiqh*; loosely, 'Islamic law and jurisprudence') in the first and second editions, respectively, of the *Encyclopaedia of Islam*.) Goldziher, in his very influential *Muhammedanische Studien* (1889–90), propounded his view that the whole genre of *ḥadīth* was not to be trusted, while Schacht, in his equally, if not more, influential *Origins of Muhammadan Jurisprudence* (1950), reinforced and extended this scepticism to include Islamic law (see further Chapter 5). Since that time, the general trend – although not without counter-voices – seems to have been to affirm this dominance of the field. David Powers, for example, in his *Studies in Qur'an and Ḥadīth* (1986), while noting the reservations of scholars such as Coulson and Azami in particular, and his own identification of certain 'fundamental weaknesses' in Schacht's work, nevertheless refers to it as 'the benchmark of all modern studies on this subject'.[1] In a similar vein, Norman Calder, in his *Studies in Early Muslim Jurisprudence* (1993), claims that 'Schacht's depiction of the stages through which Islamic law has developed, though frequently challenged, has never been seriously undermined'.[2] Shortly afterwards, Christopher Melchert, in his *Formation of the Sunni Schools of Law* (1997), wrote that Schacht

> knew the legal sources better than any predecessor among Western scholars, and his work on Islamic law … marks the greatest advance since Goldziher's. Much remains to be done, but for the early period it will be done on the basis of Schacht.[3]

Perhaps. But in that case all who try to do so will have to undo Schacht's understanding of 'the ancient schools', including the Medinan school that Mālik was presenting, and representing, in his *Muwaṭṭa'*. For Schacht, in highlighting al-Shāfi'ī's role in championing Prophetic *ḥadīth* as the gateway to the *sunna* effectively denied the role of the Prophet in the *sunna* as it was understood by the 'ancient' schools, especially the ancient school of Medina, and only allowed the two, that is, the Prophet and the *sunna*, to be united via al-Shāfiʿī's insistence on correctly attributed 'Prophetic' *ḥadīth*. But this was effectively to throw out the baby with the bath-water.

Since Schacht's time, scholars working on this area have been increasingly categorized into two opposing groups, referred to by Herbert Berg in particular as the 'skeptics' and the 'sanguines'.[4] The 'skeptics' are sceptical about whether one can accept anything on the basis of *ḥadīth*, whereas the 'sanguines' are at least open to the possibility that the *ḥadīth* contains a reasonable kernel of truth about the early history of Islam. This is not the place to go into these debates in depth. An admirable survey has been published recently by Mariam Sheibani, Amir Toft and Ahmed El Shamsy, which gives easy entry into the whole issue.[5]

Fortunately, we are not dependent solely on the *ḥadīth* record for our knowledge of the early period. In a field where even the dating of early Islam is sometimes doubted, Alan Jones's article on the papyrus PERF 558 indicates that Hijrī dating is, or at least can be, accurate: a cross-referenced date using both Greek and Arabic (Hijrī) dating indicates a 'Year 22' in Hijrī terms, thus clearly implying that something happened twenty-two years earlier, namely, the beginning of a new era that began with the Hijra.[6] The same considerations apply to epigraphic material found recently in Saudi Arabia, which yields dates such as 23, 24 (referred to as 'the time when ʿUmar died') and 91 AH,[7] as well as referring overtly to at least one of the teachers of Mālik, ʿAbd al-Raḥmān ibn Ḥarmala (for whom, see further Chapter 2). Other physical evidence that could be adduced for the history of early Islam includes not only early fragments of the Qur'an – rarely dated, but often roughly dateable on palaeographical grounds – but also physical ruins, such as those of the fortress of Kaʿb ibn al-Ashraf, or the *uṭum* (walled household) of the Banī Wāqif, or the house of ʿUrwa ibn al-Zubayr, all of which (and others) are visible in Medina to this day.

But even if we took the sceptic view, it would be counter-intuitive to throw out everything. What then, can one, or should one, retain? This is where the *Muwatta'* helps, because in it we have an indisputably early text with very strong textual credentials (see further Chapter 3). But it is, of course, not only a book of *ḥadīth* – and let us allow ourselves the description 'authentic *ḥadīth*' – but also a book that talks about the actual practice of a certain people, that is, the Practice of the People of Medina, which is understood to be based on the practice of the Prophet and his Companions, and those following them in the succeeding generations, up to and including the time of Mālik.

A further note on Euro-American sources

With three notable exceptions, the whole tenor of recent 'Western' scholarship has been very critical, and often ignorant, of traditional Muslim sources and scholarship on Mālik and/or things Mālikī. The first of these three exceptions is Umar Abd-Allah Wymann-Landgraf's *Mālik and Medina* (2013). The original PhD thesis behind his book, 'Malik's Concept of *ʿAmal* in the Light of Mālikī Legal Theory' (1978), is an excellent and extremely useful study of Mālik and his method, and underwrote much of what I said in my first book. The printed version seems to emphasize 'dissent', that is, *khilāf/ikhtilāf*, or differences of opinion, whereas it would seem closer to the mark to say, as others have said, that, in the *Muwaṭṭaʾ*, Mālik is emphasizing agreement rather than dissent.[8]

The second exception is Ahmed El Shamsy's *The Canonization of Islamic Law* (2013), whose earlier chapters masterfully summarize Mālik's attitude to the Medinan tradition of his day and present Mālik and his *Muwaṭṭaʾ* as the precursor – by way of contrast – to the new 'textual', that is, post-canonization, way of thought championed by al-Shāfiʿī. Among many points of note in El Shamsy's book, and perhaps the most relevant to our study, is his observation regarding the key link in Mālik's time between the scholars of the community and the political powers of the day, or what we might call amirate.[9]

The third of the three exceptions is the new translation of the *Muwaṭṭaʾ* by Mohammed Fadel and Connell Monette, published by Harvard University Press on behalf of the Moroccans.[10] This is prefaced by an excellent introduction which gives an overview of the book's importance, highlighting the key issues of the authenticity of the material and the authority represented by it.

In the present work, I am not overly concerned with either 'dissent' or 'canonization', as in the first two of the above three exceptions (nor am I presenting a new translation). Rather, the focus is on a pre-canonical landscape and a pre-*madhhab* ('school of law') Islam, where the dominant manifestation of the *dīn* ('religion', but with the broader sense of 'life-transaction') was in *ʿamal*, 'action', in the context of amirate. Mālik notes, for instance, that his frequently used expression *al-amru ʿindanā* ('the position with us') refers to 'what the people here have acted upon, and has become the basis for judgements [i.e. of the judiciary], and is known by both the learned and the ignorant'.[11] This context of amirate is further emphasized by various judgements in the *Muwaṭṭaʾ*. With regard to *zakāt* (the obligatory alms-tax and the third of the Five Pillars of Islam), for example, Mālik notes that the decision about who to give *zakāt* to lies with the governor (*wālī*), who may decide which category among the eight categories mentioned in the Qur'an (in Q.9:60) should be given preference in any one year, as it is also up to the leader (*imām*) to decide how much government officials collecting *zakāt* (*al-ʿāmilīna ʿalayhā*) should get for their services.[12] The interplay between scholars and political authorities is also highlighted by numerous judgements recorded by Mālik involving the caliphs and/or their governors.[13] For example, Mālik records how Zayd ibn Thābit and another of the Companions went to Marwān, the then governor of Medina, and said, 'Are you permitting usury?' to which Marwān replied, 'I seek refuge in Allah! And how is that?' The man replied, 'People are reselling the chits (*ṣukūk*) that they get for the foodstuffs at the market of al-Jār [on the Red Sea coast, not far from Medina], before taking possession of the food.' So Marwān sent out the guard (*al-ḥaras*) to collect (these chits) from people and give them back to their original owners.[14] It should be noted that this is not just about usury and its Qur'anic condemnation (Q.2:279) but also the judgement of the Prophet forbidding people from reselling foodstuffs before they had taken possession of them.[15] In other words, it is a defence of both Qur'an and *sunna*, in the context of amirate. Nor should we ignore the general point mentioned above that many of the judgements recorded by Mālik refer to 'what the people have acted upon, and has become the basis for judgements, and is known by both the learned and the ignorant'; in other words, they are judgements that have what one might call 'governmental' backing.

Of other recent work which has included significant reference to Mālik and his *Muwaṭṭaʾ*, one might feel obliged to mention Calder's *Studies in Early Muslim Jurisprudence* (1993). But, despite certain supporters, Calder's work has not stood the test of time and has generally been criticized beyond repair.[16] Brief mention should be made, however, of Jonathan Brockopp, who, more than most, has worked extensively on early 'Mālikī' texts. In an article published in 2002, Brockopp cites the following from the preface of the *Mukhtaṣar* of Abū Muṣʿab al-Zuhrī (using Brockopp's translation, unedited):

> Some claim that the people of Medina are lost, that they make legal pronouncements without foundation and they make no sense in their rulings and their legal statements But anyone whose statement depends on a verse from the Book of God which has been passed down, or a Sunnah [of] the Prophet of God, God's blessings and peace be upon him, which is followed, or [a report] transmitted on the authority of the Imāms of the Muslims, or an account of the [companions] of the Prophet of God, upon him be [peace, is indebted] to [those whom] God [has filled] with His knowledge.
>
> God chose [the people of Medina] for His Prophet to make them his helpers and He said to them: 'Take counsel with them in the affair.' And he gave them, and no other, through [the Prophet] a distinction and a knowledge which He has not given to others. In their homes was the revelation and from them arises the interpretation, and from them come the Imāms who should be emulated. And they are God's proof of His creation up to the day of judgement. The truth [of God] has no record [of application] except among them and for them. Medina is the place [to which the Prophet and his companions] emigrated and the highpoint of their community. Their influences were upon it and their rulings were made in it.
>
> ...
>
> There have come down [to us] from the Prophet of God – God's blessings and peace be upon him – two or three conflicting reports about the same matter which cannot all be observed at the same time. In this case the people of Medina act according to only one of the three reports and argue for it [in the following way]: Surely this one is according to the custom (*ʿamal*) of the Imāms of the Muslims who followed it and arranged their actions according to it. It became the generally accepted custom among them.
>
> The People of Medina say: this is how we found the custom of our area. [They argue that] their words in this regard are more trustworthy than a story related from one person to another (*qawlahum hādhā aqwā min ḥikāyati wāḥidin ʿan wāḥid*).[17]

Brockopp curiously takes this as evidence that there was no reliance on Qur'an or *sunna*, and that Abū Muṣʿab's preface is 'proof that the text was regarded as a threat to the authority of Prophet and Qur'an', and also says that Abū Muṣʿab saw his work 'as different from texts ultimately based on Qur'an and *ḥadīth*'.[18] First, this passage is so close to Malik's understanding of the position of the people of Medina (see further Chapter 4), and this understanding is so clearly based on Qur'an and *sunna* – with *sunna* not to be understood specifically as *ḥadīth*, of course, but definitely based on the authority of Prophet – that it is difficult to see what Brockopp is trying to suggest. One need only think of the chapters on business transactions (*buyūʿ*) and *qirāḍ* (a type of commenda partnership) in the *Muwaṭṭaʾ* to see how much they are based on Qur'an and *sunna*. Again and again in these chapters, Mālik is concerned to uphold the prohibitions against usury and/or uncertainty (*gharar*) in business transactions. With regard to the first, we note the Qur'anic injunction 'O you who believe, give up any remaining usury, if you are believers. If you do not, then be warned of a war from Allah and His messenger' (Q.2:278–9). Mālik says, quite unambiguously, referring to the same section in Sūrat al-Baqara: 'As for usury, it is always rejected, and neither a little or a lot of it is permitted … [This is] because Allah, the Blessed and Exalted, says in His Book "and if you repent, then you are entitled to your capital, without wronging or being wronged (Q.2:279)." '[19] This concern is backed up by frequent references to usury throughout the two chapters, including a statement recorded from ʿAbdallāh ibn Masʿūd to the effect that no one making a loan should stipulate any increase in return, even if only 'a handful of fodder (*qabḍa min ʿalaf*)'.[20]

As for *gharar*, Mālik records a *ḥadīth* expressly prohibiting it,[21] as well as other *ḥadīths* prohibiting related practices such as *muzābana* (exchanging a specific amount of a harvested crop for an unspecific amount of the same crop before harvesting e.g. dried dates for fresh dates still on the palm) and *muḥāqala* (leasing land in exchange for fresh wheat);[22] or *mulāmasa* (sales by touching e.g. a piece of cloth without examining it) and *munābadha* (sales by tossing an item between two people, without either examining the item).[23] As is the case with usury, there are frequent references to *gharar* throughout the chapter on business transactions.

It is true of course that Abū Muṣʿab's *Mukhtaṣar* is not the same as Mālik's *Muwaṭṭaʾ*, but the theoretical standpoint outlined in Abū Muṣʿab's introduction is immediately recognizable as very similar, to say the least, to Mālik's position as outlined, for example, by Qadi ʿIyāḍ in his *Madārik* (see further Chapter 4).

It is also clear from what we have mentioned above that the prohibitions against usury and *gharar*, both very evident in the Book of Sales (*Kitāb al-Buyūʿ*) in particular, are very much based on Qur'an and *sunna*, despite Brockopp's assertion to the contrary.

It is in this context that we present *Early Islam in Medina: Mālik and His* Muwaṭṭaʾ as, hopefully, a counterpoint to some of the sceptical voices and a finer tuning of some of the more sanguine ones, and as an emphatic reminder that Islam is based on actions rather than words, as in Mālik's report that al-Qāsim ibn Muḥammad (the grandson of the first Caliph Abū Bakr) used to say, 'I remember a time when people were not impressed by words,' to which Mālik adds the comment that the reference is to action (*al-ʿamal*), and that it is a person's actions that are looked at, not his words.[24]

The book is divided into five chapters. Chapter 1 forms a short introduction to Mālik's life and times and his status as the 'scholar of Medina'. Chapter 2 considers the main teachers of Mālik, with a view to outlining the intellectual and human environment in which he received his learning, and also fleshing out the otherwise often ignored names of some of the key figures in the *isnād*s (chains of authority) of the *ḥadīth*s. Chapter 3 considers some of his main students, as represented by some of the main transmitters of the *Muwaṭṭaʾ* from Mālik, as it also considers their different transmissions as an accurate preservation of his teachings – and the teachings of his teachers – to be passed down to later generations. Going beyond this primarily textual focus, Chapter 4 concentrates on the key concept of the practice (*ʿamal*) of the people of Medina and how this not only forms the backbone of Mālik's teachings but also preserves a distinctively non-textual way of viewing these teachings which contrasts with the more standard textual understanding, and transmission, of the same. Chapter 5 presents some of the conflicts that have arisen – both in ancient and modern times – around this different understanding of the practice of the early Muslim community, and, by extension, a different understanding of what constitutes the *sunna*, or normative practice, of the Prophet, and what should thus be followed by the Muslim community. A short conclusion summarizes the main thrust of the work.

1

The man and his family

Mālik is known by the honorific title of Imām Dār al-Hijra, or 'the Imam of the Abode of Emigration'. This 'Abode of Emigration' is the city of Medina in western Arabia, to which the Prophet Muhammad and his Companions emigrated after being forced to leave Mecca in the early days of the nascent Muslim community. 'Imam' is a title of respect which means, literally, 'one who goes in front, one who leads the way'. This can be either in the sense of a political leader, or someone leading others in the prayer, or – as in our present context – one who is above, or in front of, others in the excellence of his knowledge. Mālik is also known as the 'scholar (*ʿālim*) of Medina', referring to the well-known *ḥadīth* in which the Prophet said, 'The time is nigh when people will beat the livers of their camels [i.e. urge them on] in search of knowledge, but they will not find anyone more knowledgeable than the scholar of Medina' (this is related by, amongst others, Aḥmad in his *Musnad* and al-Tirmidhī in his *Ṣaḥīḥ*).[1] Imam Mālik was thus the religious leader and expert in Medina in his time, having inherited knowledge of the principles and precepts of Islam in the very place where those principles and precepts had been first formulated and acted upon by the first community of Muslims, both during the lifetime of the Prophet and in the first hundred years or so after his death.

Mālik (d. 179/795) is one of the Four Imams associated with the four main Sunni schools of law (*madhhab*s) recognized as authoritative by Muslims up until this day. These four schools are as follows: the Mālikīs, named after our imam; the Ḥanafīs, named after Imam Abū Ḥanīfa (d. 150/767); the Shāfiʿīs, named after Imam al-Shāfiʿī (d. 204/820); and the Ḥanbalīs, named after Imam Aḥmad ibn Ḥanbal (d. 241/855). The Mālikī school, or *madhhab*, is particularly dominant today in North and West Africa, although it is still represented to a lesser degree in Egypt, the Sudan and parts of Arabia. Formerly, it was also widespread in Iraq and some areas further east, but for various reasons it began to decline there until, by the end of the fifth/eleventh century, it effectively no longer had an active presence in the east of the Muslim world. In the present day, we note several newly established outliers of this *madhhab* in Europe (particularly France, Germany, Italy, Russia, Spain, Switzerland and the UK), but also in South Africa, South-East Asia (Indonesia and Malaysia) and the Americas (Mexico and the United States).

Mālik's birth

As is usual with the birthdates of individuals in the early Islamic period, when recording such events was of little importance, there is uncertainty as to the exact date of Mālik's birth. The dominant opinion, however, is that he was born either in the year 93/711 or during the caliphate of Sulaymān ibn ʿAbd al-Malik (r. 96–99/715–17) of the Umayyad dynasty.[2] There is also uncertainty about his place of birth: many sources suggest that he was born in Medina, but some specify that he was born in Dhū l-Marwa, a village lying some eight mail-stages – approximately 100 miles – to the north of Medina in the Wādī l-Qurā region.[3] However, this was considered an outlying district of Medina, since it was under Medinan political control, and so the general attribution to Medina remains valid.

Mālik's family

Mālik's full name, using the style of our sources, is Mālik ibn ('son of') Anas ibn Mālik ibn Abī ʿĀmir al-Aṣbaḥī. 'Al-Aṣbaḥī' refers to the Yemeni tribe of Dhū Aṣbaḥ, highlighting that Mālik's ancestors were originally from the Yemen. We are told that it was either his great-grandfather, Abū ʿĀmir, or his grandfather, Mālik, who moved north to Medina, becoming affiliated by invitation to the Qurayshi clan of the Banī Taym ibn Murra. We do not hear much about his mother's side of the family, except that his mother's name was al-ʿĀliya bint ('daughter of') Shurayk ibn ʿAbd al-Raḥmān ibn Shurayk al-Azdiyya, this last adjective indicating that she was from the tribe of Azd. Our sources tell us – not without a degree of pride – that Mālik was therefore of pure Arab ancestry on both his father's and his mother's side.

Mālik's great-grandfather, Abū ʿĀmir, is said to have been a Companion, although there is doubt about this as a number of key works listing the Companions do not mention him.[4] The sources note, however, that he was one of those who related *ḥadīth* from the third caliph, ʿUthmān, and he would therefore have been one of the older Successors, even if he was not a Companion. (Companions are those who met the Prophet, even if only briefly, and believed in him; Successors are Muslims who met one of the Companions, even if only briefly.) This connection with ʿUthmān is more apparent with Mālik's grandfather, Mālik ibn Abī ʿĀmir, who was one of the older Successors and a respected man of learning in Medina: not only did he relate *ḥadīth* from ʿUthmān (and from other Companions as well), but he was also involved in writing out copies of the Qur'an following ʿUthmān's decision to unify the Muslims on one written form of the text. The connection is further emphasized by reports that he was involved in the conquest of North Africa under the direct orders of ʿUthmān, and that, on ʿUthmān's death, he was one of the four people who carried the body to the grave.[5] Some *ḥadīth*s from him are included by Mālik in his book the *Muwaṭṭaʾ* (see further Chapter 2).

Mālik's grandfather, Mālik ibn Abī ʿĀmir, had four male children: Anas, the eldest (and the father of our Mālik), Uways, Nāfiʿ (known as Abū Suhayl) and al-Rabīʿ. Of these four, Nāfiʿ Abū Suhayl is particularly noted for his knowledge of *ḥadīth*, and Mālik includes a number of reports from him in the *Muwaṭṭaʾ*, including nearly all the above-mentioned *ḥadīth*s narrated from Nāfiʿ's father, Mālik ibn Abī ʿĀmir. Both al-Rabīʿ and Anas, the father of our Mālik, also appear in the sources as transmitters of *ḥadīth*, but only very infrequently.

In short, Mālik was born into a family whose forebears had settled in Medina in time to experience the full flourishing of the early Muslim community there, especially under the first years of ʿUthmān's caliphate before civil strife set in. Furthermore, although he was born two generations after ʿUthmān, he had direct access not only to the memories and experiences of his own family but also to the memories and experiences of those around him, and especially – as one interested in learning – to those of the men of knowledge in his native city.

His early life

We know little about Mālik's early life. The few reports we have suggest that he began studying early – probably in his early teens or earlier. One report, for example, tells of his mother dressing him up in the 'clothes of learning' and sending him to study under Rabīʿa, one of the main scholars of Medina at that time and possibly, by virtue of this report, Mālik's first teacher (for Rabīʿa, see further, Chapter 2). The report suggests that Mālik was young enough to have his mother help him get ready to go out and begin to study, although exactly what age he was we cannot say. Whatever his age, it seems that he quickly amassed a solid body of knowledge such that he himself was able to teach it in the mosque in Medina while still in his early twenties – 'in the lifetime of Nāfiʿ', as our sources put it.[6] (Nāfiʿ the *mawla* of Ibn 'Umar, and one of Mālik's main teachers [see further Chapter 2], died *c.* 117/735, when Mālik – assuming a birthdate of 93 AH – would have been 23 or 24 years of age.)

His children

We do not hear much about Mālik's own family life. The sources mention three sons, Yaḥyā, Muḥammad and Ḥammād, and Yaḥyā is listed as one of those who related the *Muwaṭṭaʾ* from Mālik. So, too, is a daughter named Fāṭima, who also seems to have been well versed in her father's teaching: the story is told of her standing behind the door while a student was reading out a text to her father; when he made a mistake, she tapped on the door to alert her father to the error that, it seems, had gone unnoticed.[7]

His death

Mālik died in 179/795, in Medina, where he is buried in the graveyard of al-Baqīʿ, which lies just to the east of the main mosque. Ibn Jubayr, in his *Riḥla*, mentions that the Imam's grave had a small dome over it when he visited it in the year 580/1184.[8] This, and similar domes, remained until they were razed to the ground by the Wahhābīs in 1221/1806. They were then reconstructed in the later Ottoman period, when Mālik's was one of the few graves that had a white dome over it as a mark of distinction, as was also the case with the graves of the Prophet's family, and of the caliph ʿUthmān, and several early martyrs. His grave lies next to that of Imam Nāfiʿ, the main Qur'an reciter of Medina in Mālik's later life.[9] With the entry of the Wahhābīs into the Ḥijāz a second time in 1924, and then into Medina in 1925, these domes were again demolished.[10] Now all that remains are a few stones marking these graves, including Mālik's, as a mute testimony to the excellence of those buried there.

2

His teachers

We have seen how Mālik was known as the scholar, or man of knowledge, of Medina. This knowledge, of course, was dependent on others before him. Following the practice of traditional biographers – but without intending a biography – we first consider the people from whom he gained this knowledge and then consider what this knowledge was.

Mālik had many teachers. The *Muwaṭṭaʾ* alone contains reports transmitted by him from well over ninety shaykhs, and other teachers of his are represented in other sources.

An excellent idea of these teachers can be obtained from the book *al-Tamhīd* written by the Andalusian scholar Ibn ʿAbd al-Barr (368–463/978–1070). In this book, Ibn ʿAbd al-Barr presents in alphabetical order all the scholars from whom Mālik relates Prophetic *ḥadīth* in the *Muwaṭṭaʾ*, as well as providing a commentary on each of these *ḥadīth*s. (By 'Prophetic', we mean those *ḥadīth*s that are related from the Prophet rather than what might be otherwise simply Companion or Successor *ḥadīth*s which only go back to a Companion or Successor.) All in all he includes 791 *ḥadīth*s from 98 shaykhs, ranging from those from whom Mālik relates many *ḥadīth*s to those from whom he only relates one or two. (It should be borne in mind that we are talking here only about *ḥadīth*s with either a full or partial chain of authority (*isnād*) back to the Prophet; other Prophetic *ḥadīth*s without any *isnād* i.e. what are known as *balaghāt ḥadīth*s are not included in these figures.) Of these ninety-eight shaykhs, fifteen are each the source of ten or more Prophetic *ḥadīth*s in the *Muwaṭṭaʾ*, as in Table 1 (based on Ibn ʿAbd al-Barr's figures).

These fifteen shaykhs are thus the source of nearly three-quarters (74%) of this total number of *ḥadīth*s, with the other 26 per cent being related from the remaining eighty-three shaykhs. From this it is clear that, while transmitting

Table 1 Mālik's Main Teachers

	Name of shaykh	No. of *ḥadīths* in the *Muw.*
1	Ibn Shihāb al-Zuhrī	131
2	Nāfiʿ, the *mawlā* of Ibn ʿUmar	80
3	Yaḥyā ibn Saʿīd al-Anṣārī	77
4	Hishām ibn ʿUrwa	57
5	Abū l-Zinād	54
6	Zayd ibn Aslam	51
7	ʿAbdallāh ibn Abī Bakr ibn Ḥazm	26
8	ʿAbdallāh ibn Dīnār	26
9	Isḥāq ibn ʿAbdallāh ibn Abī Ṭalḥa	15
10	Sālim, Abū l-Nadr	15
11	Sumayy, the *mawlā* of Abū Bakr ibn ʿAbd al-Raḥmān	13
12	Rabīʿa ibn ʿAbd al-Raḥmān	12
13	Suhayl al-Sammān	10
14	ʿAbd al-Raḥmān ibn al-Qāsim	10
15	al-ʿAlāʾ ibn ʿAbd al-Raḥmān	10
		= 587
16–98	other shaykhs	204
	TOTAL	791

from many individuals, a large proportion of Mālik's material derives from a small number of particularly important teachers.

In the sections that follow, we take a brief look at each of these fifteen shaykhs, as well as a few others of particular interest, paying particular attention, where appropriate, to what has been recorded from Mālik about them. Taken together, they give an excellent idea of the intellectual environment in which Mālik received his learning, and also of the strong ties, both intellectual and familial, that existed between these men and many of the key Companions in Medina.

1. Ibn Shihāb al-Zuhrī

As can be seen from the above table, by far the largest number of *ḥadīth*s related from any one shaykh in the *Muwaṭṭaʾ* are those related from Ibn Shihāb al-Zuhrī.

Ibn Shihāb was born around the year 51/671 and died (on his estate of Shaghb and Badā in the north of the Ḥijāz) in the year 124/742. He was considered the best of the scholars in Medina during the time of the Umayyad caliph Hishām ibn ʿAbd al-Malik (r. 105–25/724–43). It is recorded that, of the people of the generation before Ibn Shihāb, three scholars were particularly important: Saʿīd ibn al-Musayyab, ʿUrwa ibn al-Zubayr and ʿUbaydallāh ibn ʿAbdallāh. Saʿīd ibn al-Musayyab was the one with the most knowledge of the judgements of the Prophet and the first three caliphs after him, and the one with the most knowledge of *fiqh* (loosely, 'Islamic law and jurisprudence') and the practices of the Muslims handed down by the people; ʿUrwa ibn al-Zubayr was the one with the most knowledge of *ḥadīth*; and if anyone wanted a spring of knowledge to burst forth, he only had to ask ʿUbaydallāh ibn ʿAbdallāh. Ibn Shihāb gathered the knowledge of these three in addition to his own knowledge.[1] Mālik said of him, 'I have only ever seen one person who was a scholar of both *ḥadīth* and *fiqh* – Ibn Shihāb.'[2] Ibn Shihāb was known for his prodigious memory as well as the breadth and depth of his learning. It is related that Mālik once said,

> Ibn Shihāb told us forty *ḥadīth*s, and I was unsure about one of them. I waited for him and, when he was leaving, I took hold of the reins of his mule and asked him about the *ḥadīth* that I was unsure about. He said, 'Didn't I tell it to you?' I said, 'Yes, but I am unsure about it.' He said, 'Transmission is not what it used to be! Let go of the reins of my mule.' So I let go of them, and he went on his way.[3]

In another version, Ibn Shihāb replied, 'I have never had to ask anyone to repeat a *ḥadīth*!'[4] In a report from Mālik's contemporary, ʿAbd al-ʿAzīz ibn Abī Salama al-Mājishūn, Ibn Shihāb said,

> I have never written down anything. I was put in charge of [the collection of] *zakāt* and so I went to Sālim ibn ʿAbdallāh [i.e. the grandson of the caliph ʿUmar, who had a written document about *zakāt*], and he brought out for me the document about *zakāt* and read it out to me and I memorized it. I also went to Ibn Ḥazm [i.e. Abū Bakr ibn Ḥazm, the grandson of the Companion ʿAmr ibn Ḥazm, who had received a written document about blood money from the Prophet] and he read out to me the document about blood-money and I memorized it.[5]

(The contents of both documents are referred to in the *Muwaṭṭaʾ*.)[6]

It was during Ibn Shihāb's lifetime – and, it could be argued, to a large extent due to his activities – that there was a shift away from the earlier practice of simply memorising *ḥadīth* ('knowledge') to one where it became increasingly normal to write it down as well. We hear of him being initially averse to writing down *ḥadīth* – 'I never used to write anything down on these slates!' – but by the end of his life, at caliphal insistence, he not only allowed it but also earned the accolade of being the first person to make a comprehensive collection of *ḥadīth*.[7] Indeed, it was this shift from the purely oral transmission of 'knowledge' to parallel oral and written versions that was to result, in the generation after Ibn Shihāb, in the production of 'books' such as Mālik's *Muwaṭṭa*ʾ. (We return to the significance of this in Chapter 3.)

Ibn Shihāb's close association with various Umayyad governors and caliphs has been the occasion of some criticism by certain scholars, both in his own time and more recently on the presumption that association with rulers puts a question mark over a scholar's independence and integrity.[8] However, at the same time we should recognize that, in a fully functioning Muslim society, scholars and governors need to be working in close tandem in order for Islamic law to be put into practice. It is impossible, for example, to administer the collection of *zakāt* – the Third Pillar of Islam – without the direct involvement of the political authorities, since it is the political leader who is under Qur'anic command to undertake this collection.[9] At the same time, people of knowledge are necessary in order to advise him and his appointees on the correct amounts to be taken from the various categories of wealth on which *zakāt* is due. It is therefore not surprising to hear, as above, of Ibn Shihāb being appointed as a *zakāt* collector, since this, far from being the opprobrious act of 'tax collection', as some modern scholars have supposed, is actually part of the necessary and praiseworthy implementation of the law. Thus, while it is accepted that Ibn Shihāb was associated with the Umayyad government in various capacities, the judgement of his younger contemporary al-Awzāʿī (d. 157/774) seems to reflect the correct balance: 'Ibn Shihāb never ingratiated himself to any ruler when going in to see him, and I never met anyone among the Successors during the caliphate of Hishām [ibn ʿAbd al-Malik; r. 105–25/724–43] who was more knowledgeable in *fiqh* than he was.'[10]

Ibn Shihāb and the Seven (or Ten) Jurists of Medina

Ibn Shihāb was of the generation of the Younger Successors, that is, those who had met Companions and thus come under the category of Successors, but most of whose contacts were with the Older Successors. Of these Older Successors, special mention should be made of the Seven – or, as Ibn ʿAbd al-Barr allows, the Ten – Jurists of Medina. Lists of exactly who these seven, or ten, were vary – nor should we expect exactitude when such lists of 'seven' or 'ten' are mentioned in our sources – but Ibn ʿAbd al-Barr mentions a report in which the following nine names are specifically mentioned:

1. Saʿīd (ibn al-Musayyab)
2. Abū Salama ibn ʿAbd al-Raḥmān (ibn ʿAwf)
3. al-Qāsim ibn Muḥammad (ibn Abī Bakr)
4. Sālim ibn ʿAbdallāh (ibn ʿUmar)
5. ʿUrwa ibn al-Zubayr
6. Sulaymān ibn Yasār
7. ʿUbaydallāh ibn ʿAbdallāh (ibn ʿUtba ibn Masʿūd)
8. Qabīṣa ibn Dhuʾayb
9. Abān ibn ʿUthmān (ibn ʿAffān).

The tenth, Ibn ʿAbd al-Barr explains, was missing from the handwritten version of the report in question but is, in his opinion, either Khārija ibn Zayd (ibn Thābit) or Abū Bakr ibn ʿAbd al-Raḥmān ibn al-Ḥārith ibn Hishām.[11] (Elsewhere, Ibn ʿAbd al-Barr lists the Ten as Saʿīd, Abū Salama, ʿUrwa, al-Qāsim, Sālim, Abū Bakr, ʿUbaydallāh, Sulaymān, Khārija and Qabīṣa, that is, the above eleven names excluding Abān ibn ʿUthmān.)[12]

Abū l-Zinād (one of Mālik's main teachers; see further below) was asked who were the seven he was referring to when he said 'The Seven told me', and he said, 'Saʿīd ibn al-Musayyab, ʿUrwa ibn al-Zubayr, Abū Bakr ibn ʿAbd al-Raḥmān ibn al-Ḥārith ibn Hishām, al-Qāsim ibn Muḥammad, ʿUbaydallāh ibn ʿAbdallāh ibn ʿUtba ibn Masʿūd, Khārija ibn Zayd ibn Thābit, and Sulaymān ibn Yasār.'[13] It is these seven that have become standardized as the Seven Jurists of Medina.

Of the above-mentioned ten – or eleven – jurists, five feature as particularly important sources for Ibn Shihāb's *ḥadīth*s in the *Muwaṭṭaʾ*. These five are the following:

(i) Saʿīd ibn al-Musayyab (or 'al-Musayyib') (d. *c.* 94/713). Saʿīd was considered the most knowledgeable of the scholars of Medina after the deaths of ʿAbdallāh ibn ʿUmar (the caliph ʿUmar's son) and Ibn ʿAbbās. He was known as the 'transmitter of ʿUmar' because of his extensive knowledge of the judgements and decisions of ʿUmar.[14] Mālik said of him, emphasizing Saʿīd's knowledge of ʿUmar's judgements, 'I have heard that ʿAbdallāh ibn ʿUmar would contact Saʿīd ibn al-Musayyab to ask him certain things about ʿUmar.'[15] Mālik also said, 'Ibn Shihāb's *fatwā*s and opinions were based on what he learnt from Sālim [ibn ʿAbdallāh ibn ʿUmar] and Saʿīd ibn al-Musayyab.'[16]

In the *Muwaṭṭaʾ*, Mālik transmits seventeen Prophetic *ḥadīth*s from Ibn al-Musayyab via Ibn Shihāb.

(ii) ʿUrwa ibn al-Zubayr (d. *c.* 94/713). ʿUrwa was the younger brother of the famous Companion, and one-time caliph of the Ḥijāz, ʿAbdallāh ibn al-Zubayr. ʿUrwa's mother was Asmāʾ, the daughter of the first caliph Abū Bakr and sister of ʿĀʾisha, the wife of the Prophet, and a large proportion of ʿUrwa's transmitted material comes through his maternal aunt ʿĀʾisha.

Whereas Saʿīd was considered to be the most knowledgeable of the Medinan jurists with regard to the judgements of the Messenger and the first three caliphs after him, ʿUrwa ibn al-Zubayr was considered to be the most knowledgeable of them with regard to *ḥadīth*, that is, formal reports. Ibn Shihāb said that he studied under Saʿīd ibn al-Musayyab for nine years, considering no one else to be a man of knowledge, but then afterwards spent time with ʿUrwa and found him to be 'an ocean that no amount of dipping into would muddy'.[17]

In the *Muwaṭṭaʾ*, Mālik transmits fifteen Prophetic *ḥadīth*s from ʿUrwa via Ibn Shihāb.

(iii) ʿUbaydallāh ibn ʿAbdallāh ibn ʿUtba ibn Masʿūd (d. *c.* 98/716). ʿUbaydallāh ibn ʿAbdallāh was a poet as well as a jurist. Ibn ʿAbd al-Barr says of him: 'From the time of the Companions up until now there has been no jurist, as far as I know, that was more gifted at poetry, nor any poet that had a better knowledge of jurisprudence.'[18] Ibn Shihāb said of him, 'I never saw anyone who spoke better Arabic than him.'[19]

In the *Muwaṭṭaʾ*, Mālik transmits eleven Prophetic *ḥadīth*s from ʿUbaydallāh ibn ʿAbdallāh via Ibn Shihāb.

(iv) Abū Salama ibn ʿAbd al-Raḥmān ibn ʿAwf (d. 94/713 or 104/722). Abū Salama was the son of the famous Companion ʿAbd al-Raḥmān ibn ʿAwf. He was judge of Medina at the time when Saʿīd ibn al-ʿĀṣī was governor there during the caliphate of Muʿāwiya (r. 41–60/661–80). Abū Isḥāq (al-Shīrāzī?) said of him, 'Abū Salama in his time was better than [ʿAbdallāh] ibn ʿUmar in his time.'[20]

In the *Muwaṭṭaʾ*, Mālik transmits twelve Prophetic *ḥadīth*s from Abū Salama via Ibn Shihāb (including four shared with Saʿīd ibn al-Musayyab).

(v) Sālim ibn ʿAbdallāh (d. *c*. 106/724). Sālim was the son of the famous Companion ʿAbdallāh ibn ʿUmar (by a slave girl of his) and grandson of the second caliph ʿUmar. It is said that Sālim was the most like his father of all his children and that his father was the most like *his* father of all *his* children. Sālim is described as being particularly devout (*nāsik*), indicated also by his wearing wool. It is also said that (like Mālik) he never left Medina.[21]

In the *Muwaṭṭaʾ*, Mālik transmits nine Prophetic *ḥadīth*s from Sālim via Ibn Shihāb.

The other six names mentioned as being of the 'Ten' Jurists are the following:

(vi) Al-Qāsim ibn Muḥammad ibn Abī Bakr (d. 106/724, or 'in the caliphate of Yazīd ibn ʿAbd al-Malik' (r. 101–5/720–4)). Al-Qāsim was the grandson of the first caliph Abū Bakr. His father Muḥammad was killed when al-Qāsim was still young and he grew up as an orphan under the tutelage of his paternal aunt ʿĀʾisha. Mālik said of him, 'Al-Qāsim was one of the jurists of this community.'[22] The famous Iraqi scholar Muḥammad ibn Sīrīn said, 'At the time al-Qāsim ibn Muḥammad died there was no-one that people were more pleased with than him.' [ʿAbdallāh] ibn ʿAwn said, 'I saw three people the like of whom I have never seen: Ibn Sīrīn in Iraq, al-Qāsim ibn Muḥammad in the Ḥijāz, and Rajāʾ ibn Ḥaywa in Syria.'[23]

In the *Muwaṭṭaʾ*, Mālik transmits only one Companion *ḥadīth* from al-Qāsim ibn Muḥammad via Ibn Shihāb (although their names occur twice as co-reporters for shared opinions). (This is in a context of fifty-two reports altogether in the *Muwaṭṭaʾ* either from or about al-Qāsim ibn Muḥammad.)

(vii) Sulaymān ibn Yasār (d. *c*. 100/718). Sulaymān ibn Yasār was a *mukātab* slave belonging to Maymūna, the wife of the Prophet, and was manumitted by her, as were his three brothers.[24] Mālik said of him, 'Sulaymān ibn Yasār was one of the most learned men among us after Saʿīd ibn al-Musayyab.'[25] He also said of him, 'Sulaymān ibn Yasār was the most knowledgeable man that people relied upon (*kāna mulzaman*) after Saʿīd ibn al-Musayyab, and the two of them would very often agree in their opinions. If anyone raised their voice or said anything bad in his gathering, he would get up and leave.'[26]

In addition to his teaching activities, Sulaymān was put in charge of the market of Medina for a year during the governorate of ʿUmar ibn ʿAbd al-ʿAzīz (87–94/706–13) and the caliphate of al-Walīd ibn ʿAbd al-Malik (r. 86–96/705–15).[27]

In the *Muwaṭṭaʾ*, Mālik transmits two Prophetic *ḥadīth*s from Sulaymān via Ibn Shihāb.

(viii) Abū Bakr ibn ʿAbd al-Raḥmān ibn al-Ḥārith ibn Hishām (d. 94/713). Abū Bakr ibn ʿAbd al-Raḥmān was known as the 'monk of Quraysh' (*rāhib Quraysh*) because of the large amount of time he spent in prayer and worship. Mālik said of him, 'I have not heard of any of the Successors doing *iʿtikāf* [retreat in a mosque] except for Abū Bakr ibn ʿAbd al-Raḥmān. This was, I think, because of its difficulty.'[28]

In the *Muwaṭṭaʾ*, Mālik transmits two Prophetic *ḥadīth*s from Abū Bakr ibn ʿAbd al-Raḥmān via Ibn Shihāb.

(ix) Qabīṣa ibn Dhuʾayb (d. 86/705 or 87/708). Qabīṣa was praised by Ibn Shihāb as 'one of the scholars of this community'.[29] However, he features far less frequently as an authority in the *Muwaṭṭaʾ* than the other Seven, or Ten, Jurists.

Mālik transmits only one Prophetic *ḥadīth* from him in the *Muwaṭṭaʾ*, which is via Ibn Shihāb.

(x) Abān ibn ʿUthmān (d. before 105/724). Abān was the son of the third caliph ʿUthmān. He was appointed governor of Medina in the year 76/695 during the caliphate of ʿAbd al-Malik (r. 65–86/685–705). There are various reports in the *Muwaṭṭaʾ* about judgements made by Abān as governor, but Mālik only transmits one Prophetic *ḥadīth* related from him in the *Muwaṭṭaʾ*. (None of these are related via Ibn Shihāb.)

(xi) Khārija ibn Zayd ibn Thābit (d. *c.* 99/717). Khārija was the son of the famous Companion Zayd ibn Thābit. He is mentioned only three times in the *Muwaṭṭaʾ*, twice as the vehicle for judgements of his father – one of which Mālik relates from Khārija's nephew and Zayd's grandson, Saʿīd ibn Sulaymān ibn Zayd ibn Thābit – and once as an authority in his own right. (None of these are related via Ibn Shihāb.)

We may further note that, of the 120 Prophetic *ḥadīth*s in the *Muwaṭṭaʾ* where Ibn Shihāb's direct source is named, 13 are related directly from seven Companions, while the other 107 come from thirty-three Tābiʿīn. In other words, a small portion of his material is transmitted directly from Companions, but the majority of it is transmitted from other Tābiʿīn. As we have seen, of these Tābiʿīn, pride of place goes to four of the Seven/Ten Jurists, namely Saʿīd ibn al-Musayyab (seventeen *ḥadīth*s), ʿUrwa ibn al-Zubayr (fifteen *ḥadīth*s), Abū Salama (twelve *ḥadīth*s, four of which are shared with Saʿīd) and ʿUbaydallāh ibn ʿAbdallāh (eleven *ḥadīth*s). Of these four men, it is related that Ibn Shihāb said, 'I met four oceans of knowledge: Saʿīd ibn al-Musayyab, ʿUrwa ibn al-Zubayr, ʿUbaydallāh ibn ʿAbdallāh, and Abū Salama ibn ʿAbd al-Raḥmān.'[30]

As we have seen, Ibn Shihāb also transmits *ḥadīth*s in the *Muwaṭṭaʾ* from at least four of the other Seven/Ten Jurists, namely Sālim ibn ʿAbdallāh (nine *ḥadīth*s), Abū Bakr ibn ʿAbd al-Raḥmān (two *ḥadīth*s), Sulaymān ibn Yasār (two *ḥadīth*s) and Qabīṣa (one *ḥadīth*).

Other noteworthy teachers of Ibn Shihāb include ʿAlī ibn al-Ḥusayn ('Zayn al-ʿĀbidīn'), the grandson of the fourth caliph ʿAlī ibn Abī Ṭālib, from whom he relates three *ḥadīth*s in the *Muwaṭṭaʾ*, and ʿAbdallāh and al-Ḥasan, grandsons of ʿAlī through al-Ḥusayn's half-brother, Muḥammad ibn al-Ḥanafiyya, from whom he relates one *ḥadīth* in the *Muwaṭṭaʾ*.

As can be seen, many of these teachers of Ibn Shihāb were the direct descendants of well-known and respected Companions, such as ʿUrwa and al-Qāsim, who were both grandsons of the first caliph Abū Bakr; Sālim, who was grandson of the second caliph ʿUmar and son of the famous Companion ʿAbdallāh ibn ʿUmar; ʿAlī ibn al-Ḥusayn, ʿAbdallāh ibn al-Ḥanafiyya and his brother al-Ḥasan ibn al-Ḥanafiyya, who were all grandsons of the fourth caliph ʿAlī ibn Abī Ṭālib; and Abū Salama, who was the son of the famous Companion ʻAbd al-Rahmān ibn ʻAwf. The same, of course, applies to others amongst the Seven/Ten Jurists, such as Abān, the son of the third caliph ʿUthmān, and Khārija, the son of the famous Companion Zayd ibn Thābit. As mentioned above, Ibn ʿAbd al-Barr's figures include only Prophetic *ḥadīth*s, of which he includes 131. Ibn Shihāb is also the source for many other reports in the *Muwaṭṭaʾ*. A search of a digital copy of the *Muwaṭṭaʾ*, using perhaps a slightly different understanding of what constitutes a Prophetic *ḥadīth*, yielded the following results: of a total of 280 reports mentioning Ibn Shihāb, at least

123 (44%) – rather than 131 – are Prophetic *ḥadīth*s; 92 (33%) appear to be Companion *ḥadīth*s; and the remaining 65 (23%) are from Successors, with 45 of these 65 being from Ibn Shihāb as an authority in his own right. It should also be noted that, in the vast majority of instances, Mālik relates from Ibn Shihāb directly, but on five occasions he does so indirectly (via Ziyād ibn Saʿd (twice), ʿUthmān ibn Ḥafṣ ibn ʿUmar ibn Khalda (twice) and Yaḥyā ibn Saʿīd).

This, then, gives us an idea of the intellectual environment in which Ibn Shihāb, Mālik's main teacher, received his learning.

2. Nāfiʿ, the *mawlā* ('freed slave') of Ibn ʿUmar (d. 117/735)

Mālik relates eighty *musnad ḥadīth*s from Nāfiʿ in the *Muwaṭṭa*ʾ, sixty-six (83%) of which are via his patron (*mawlā*), ʿAbdallāh ibn ʿUmar, the Companion and famous son of the second caliph ʿUmar. This *isnād* ('chain of authority') of Mālik, from Nāfiʿ, from ʿAbdallāh ibn ʿUmar, from the Prophet, is known as the 'golden chain' of authority, because of its shortness and the excellence of each of its individual links. Mālik said, emphasizing the reliability of Nāfiʿ, 'If I heard a *ḥadīth* from Nāfiʿ, I wasn't worried if I didn't hear it from anyone else.'[31] Among the other fourteen *ḥadīth*s are one from al-Qāsim ibn Muḥammad (from ʿĀʾisha), one from Sulaymān ibn Yasār and one related from Ibn ʿUmar's son Zayd, from ʿAbdallāh ibn ʿAbd al-Rahmān ibn Abī Bakr, that is, from a grandson of ʿUmar from a grandson of Abū Bakr.

Also included in the *Muwaṭṭa*ʾ are a further 152 reports from Nāfiʿ from or about ʿAbdallāh ibn ʿUmar, that is, where Ibn ʿUmar is effectively cited as the final authority. A further thirteen reports cite 'higher' authorities, including ten from or about Ibn ʿUmar's father, ʿUmar. There are also two *ḥadīth*s from Ibn ʿUmar via Ibn ʿUmar's wife, Ṣafiyya bint Abī ʿUbayd, and a further five reports from her, including one about her father-in-law ʿUmar and one about her sisters-in-law Ḥafṣa and Fāṭima. In addition, Mālik transmits three reports from Nāfiʿ which he relates via Nāfiʿ's son, Abū Bakr.

It is readily apparent from the above that, as Mālik noted, Nāfiʿ was the transmitter of a great deal of knowledge from Ibn ʿUmar.[32]

With regard to the Seven/Ten Jurists, Nāfiʿ relates four reports from Ibn ʿUmar's son Sālim, as well as four reports (including one Prophetic *ḥadīth*) from Sulaymān ibn Yasār and one Prophetic *ḥadīth* from al-Qāsim ibn Muḥammad.

3. Yaḥyā ibn Saʿīd al-Anṣārī (d. 143/760)

Yaḥyā ibn Saʿīd's grandfather, Qays, was a Companion. Yaḥyā ibn Saʿīd was appointed judge of Medina during the governorate of Yūsuf ibn Muḥammad al-Thaqafī in the time of al-Walīd ibn Yazīd ibn ʿAbd al-Malik (r. 125–6/743–4). He later went to Iraq where he was appointed judge – of al-Hāshimiyya, a town built by the caliph al-Saffāḥ in Kufa – by Abū Jaʿfar al-Manṣūr (r. 136–58/754–75). Having not been well off, his fortunes changed for the better after Abū Jaʿfar made him judge. He himself, however, didn't change and he remained generous with his money. He was once asked about this and he said, 'If a person is strong in himself (*nafsuhu wāḥida*), money won't change him.'[33] On one occasion he arranged for Rabīʿa (another of Mālik's shaykhs; see below) to go to Ifrīqiyya to collect some inheritance for him, and, when Rabīʿa returned with 500 dinars, he divided the sum equally between himself and Rabīʿa.[34]

Mālik relates seventy-seven *musnad ḥadīths* from Yaḥyā ibn Saʿīd in the *Muwaṭṭaʾ*. As with Ibn Shihāb, Yaḥyā ibn Saʿīd relates a number of *ḥadīths* from the Seven/Ten Jurists, including nine from Saʿīd ibn al-Musayyab, one from Abū Salama, four from Sulaymān ibn Yasār and one from al-Qāsim ibn Muḥammad. Another important source for him was ʿAmra bint ʿAbd al-Rahmān, from who he relates seven *ḥadīths*, six of which are from ʿĀʾisha (one of ʿAmra's main sources).

4. Hishām ibn ʿUrwa (d. 146/763)

Hishām's father was ʿUrwa ibn al-Zubayr, who, as noted above, was one of the Seven/Ten Jurists of Medina and younger brother of the famous Companion, and one-time caliph of the Ḥijāz, ʿAbdallāh ibn al-Zubayr. As mentioned earlier, ʿUrwa's mother was Asmāʾ, the daughter of the first caliph Abū Bakr and sister of ʿĀʾisha, and so Hishām was a great-grandson of Abū Bakr. Hishām's mother was a slave girl from Khurasan.

Nearly all the Prophetic *ḥadīth*s (fifty-three out of fifty-seven) from Hishām in the *Muwaṭṭaʾ* are related from his father ʿUrwa, and nearly half of these (twenty-three) are related by ʿUrwa from his aunt, ʿĀʾisha. Hishām also transmits from other family members, such as his cousins ʿAbbād ibn ʿAbdallāh ibn al-Zubayr and Fāṭima bint al-Mundhir ibn al-Zubayr (who was also his wife). He also transmits various Companion *ḥadīth*s – again, on the authority of his father – as well as a number of reports of his father's own opinions.

5. Abū l-Zinād ibn Dhakwān (d. 130/748)

Abū l-Zinād's father, Dhakwān, was a *mawlā* of Ramla, the wife of the third caliph ʿUthmān ibn ʿAffān (although some say he was the *mawlā* of ʿUthmān's daughter, ʿĀʾisha, or of ʿUthmān himself). Abū l-Zinād was one of those who gave *fatwā* in Medina, and he and Rabīʿa (see below) were considered the two jurists of Medina in their time, with many considering Abū l-Zinād to be the more knowledgeable of the two. Mālik said, 'Abū l-Zinād used to have a study circle by himself in the mosque of the Messenger of Allah, may Allah bless him and grant him peace.' He acted as secretary (*kātib*) for ʿAbd al-Ḥamīd ibn ʿAbd al-Raḥmān ibn Zayd ibn al-Khaṭṭāb, the governor of Kufa during the caliphate of ʿUmar ibn ʿAbd al-ʿAzīz (r. 99–101/717–20), and also as secretary for Khālid ibn ʿAbd al-Malik ibn al-Ḥārith ibn al-Ḥakam, the governor of Medina from 114–118/732–736, during the caliphate of Hishām ibn ʿAbd al-Malik (r. 105–25/724–43). In both instances he was in charge of the financial affairs of the treasury (*bayt al-māl*).[35]

It is related that he went to see the caliph, Hishām ibn ʿAbd al-Malik, with the details of the financial accounts of Medina and sat with Hishām in the company of Ibn Shihāb. Hishām asked Ibn Shihāb what the month was in which ʿUthmān would give the people of Medina their stipends and Ibn Shihāb said that he didn't know. (Abū l-Zinād commented, 'We used to think that Ibn Shihāb would never be asked about anything without him having knowledge of it.') Hishām then asked Abū l-Zinād, and he said, 'In [the month of] Muḥarram.'[36]

Mālik relates fifty-four *musnad ḥadīths* from Abū l-Zinād in the *Muwaṭṭa'*, all of which are from al-A'raj, from Abū Hurayra. The *Muwaṭṭa'* also includes twelve other Companion and Successor *ḥadīths* transmitted by Abū l-Zinād from or via other authorities, including four from Sa'īd ibn al-Musayyab, three from or via Sulaymān ibn Yasār, two via Abū Salama and one via Khārija.

6. Zayd ibn Aslam (d. 136/754)

Zayd's father, Aslam, was a *mawlā* of the second caliph 'Umar who had been brought to Medina as a captive after the battle of 'Ayn al-Tamr during the caliphate of Abū Bakr (r. 11–13/632–4). Aslam was considered one of the best of the *mawālī* in terms of his knowledge and behaviour, and his son followed in his footsteps.

Zayd ibn Aslam was said to be the most learned of the people of Medina with regard to interpretation of the Qur'an after Muḥammad ibn Ka'b al-Quraẓī. Mālik said of him, 'Zayd ibn Aslam was a man of knowledge who feared Allah. He would act kindly towards me (*yanbasiṭu ilayya*), and would say, "Son of Adam, fear Allah and people will love you, whether they want to or not." '[37] Zayd's grandson (Zayd ibn 'Abd al-Rahman ibn Zayd ibn Aslam) said that when Mālik compiled the *Muwaṭṭa'*, he put the *ḥadīths* of Zayd ibn Aslam at the end of the various chapters. When he asked Mālik about this, he said, 'They are like a lamp which casts light on what is before them.'[38]

Mālik relates fifty-one Prophetic *ḥadīths* from Zayd ibn Aslam in the *Muwaṭṭa'*. Nearly half of these (twenty-three) are from 'Aṭā' ibn Yasār, the brother of Sulaymān ibn Yasār. ('Aṭā' and Sulaymān – along with two other brothers – were the *mawālī* of Maymūna, the wife of the Prophet; Sulaymān was considered to be the one with the best knowledge of *fiqh*, whereas 'Aṭā' had the best knowledge of *ḥadīth*.) Other shaykhs of Zayd ibn Aslam mentioned in the *isnāds* of his *ḥadīths* include his father Aslam (two *ḥadīths* and various Companion reports), his brother Khālid (one report about 'Umar) and Sa'īd ibn al-Musayyab (one *ḥadīth*).

7. ʿAbdallāh ibn Abī Bakr (ibn Muḥammad ibn ʿAmr) ibn Ḥazm (d. *c.* 135/752)

ʿAbdallāh's father, Abū Bakr ibn Ḥazm, was appointed judge of Medina during the governorship of ʿUmar ibn ʿAbd al-ʿAzīz (*c.* 87–*c.* 93/*c.* 706–*c.* 712). When ʿUmar ibn ʿAbd al-ʿAzīz became caliph (r. 99–101/717–20), he appointed Abū Bakr ibn Ḥazm as governor of Medina. Mālik said of Abū Bakr ibn Ḥazm,

> There was no-one among us in Medina who had more knowledge about giving judgement (*ʿilm al-qaḍāʾ*) than Abū Bakr ibn Muḥammad ibn ʿAmr ibn Ḥazm. He was appointed governor by ʿUmar ibn ʿAbd al-ʿAzīz, who wrote to him telling him to write down knowledge [i.e. *ḥadīth*s] from ʿAmra bint ʿAbd al-Raḥmān and al-Qāsim ibn Muḥammad, and he wrote it down for him. No other Anṣārī was ever appointed governor of Medina other than Abū Bakr ibn Ḥazm. He was also a judge.[39]

Abū Bakr's grandfather, ʿAmr ibn Ḥazm, was a well-known Companion. He is especially known for the written document mentioned earlier that was entrusted to him by the Prophet to the people of the Yemen, which contained details about various legal issues, especially blood money (and which is referred to in the *Muwaṭṭaʾ*).

Mālik said that (ʿUmāra?) Ibn Ghaziyya was once asked by Ibn Shihāb about those who were giving *fatwā* in Medina and he said, 'There is no-one among them like ʿAbdallāh ibn Abī Bakr, and he would be much better known if it were not that his father is still alive.'[40]

Mālik relates twenty-six *ḥadīth*s from ʿAbdallāh ibn Abī Bakr in the *Muwaṭṭaʾ*, ten of which are from his father. Five *ḥadīth*s are related from the above-mentioned ʿAmra bint ʿAbd al-Raḥmān, three of them directly and two via his father. Among the other eleven *ḥadīth*s are two from ʿAbd al-Malik ibn Abī Bakr ibn ʿAbd al-Raḥmān ibn al-Ḥārith ibn Hishām, that is, the son of the Abū Bakr who is one of the Seven/Ten Jurists.

Among Abū Bakr ibn Ḥazm's sons, ʿAbdallāh was the most renowned for his knowledge of *ḥadīth*. Another son, Muḥammad – who, like his father, was a judge – is also mentioned as an authority by Mālik in the *Muwaṭṭaʾ*, where he transmits three reports from him: a Prophetic *ḥadīth*, via his father Abū Bakr, and two reports from ʿUmar, one of which is also via his father.

8. ʿAbdallāh ibn Dīnār (d. 127/744 or 131/748)

ʿAbdallāh ibn Dīnār was, like Nāfiʿ, a *mawlā* of ʿAbdallāh ibn ʿUmar. Mālik relates twenty-six Prophetic *ḥadīth*s from him, most of which (twenty-two) are via his patron Ibn ʿUmar. Of the other four, two are via Sulaymān ibn Yasār and two via Abū Ṣāliḥ al-Sammān, the father of one of Mālik's main shaykhs (see below).

9. Isḥāq ibn ʿAbdallāh ibn Abī Ṭalḥa (d. 132/749 or 134/751)

Isḥāq was considered the most knowledgeable and most reliable of a number of brothers who all transmitted *ḥadīth*. His grandfather, Abū Ṭalḥa, was one of the older Companions. According to al-Wāqidī, there was no one that Mālik would put before Isḥāq ibn ʿAbdallāh ibn Abī Ṭalḥa with regard to *ḥadīth*.[41]

Mālik relates fifteen *ḥadīth*s from Isḥāq ibn ʿAbdallāh ibn Abī Ṭalḥa in the *Muwaṭṭaʾ*, ten of which are from the Companion Anas ibn Mālik, who was Isḥāq's uncle. (Anas and ʿAbdallāh ibn Abī Ṭalḥa were sons of the same mother, Anas by her first marriage and 'Abdallah by her second.) One of the other five is related by Isḥāq from his wife, Ḥumayda bint Abī ʿUbayda. He also relates four Companion reports from Anas.

10. Sālim, Abū l-Naḍr (d. 133/750 or 130/747)

Sālim, more commonly known as Abū l-Naḍr, was the *mawlā* of ʿUmar ibn ʿUbaydallāh ibn Maʿmar al-Taymī, one of the notables of Quraysh under whom Abū l-Naḍr worked as a secretary. ʿUmar's grandfather, Maʿmar, was a Companion and cousin of Abū Quḥāfa, Abū Bakr's father.[42] Mālik described Abū l-Naḍr as a man of excellence, intelligence and worship.[43]

Mālik relates fifteen Prophetic *ḥadīth*s from Abū l-Naḍr in the *Muwaṭṭaʾ*, six of which are via the Seven/Ten Jurists (three via Abū Salama, two via Sulaymān ibn Yasār and one via ʿUbaydallāh ibn ʿAbdallāh ibn ʿUtba).

11. Sumayy, the *mawlā* of Abū Bakr (d. 130/747)

Sumayy was the *mawlā* of Abū Bakr ibn ʿAbd al-Raḥmān ibn al-Ḥārith ibn Hishām, one of the Seven/Ten Jurists of Medina.[44]

Mālik relates thirteen Prophetic *ḥadīth*s from Sumayy in the *Muwaṭṭaʾ* (although, since one of them effectively combines three different *ḥadīth*s, Ibn ʿAbd al-Barr allows that one could consider them fifteen *ḥadīth*s altogether). Of these, four are from his patron Abū Bakr ibn ʿAbd al-Raḥmān. All the others (nine, or eleven) are from Abū Ṣāliḥ al-Sammān (the father of Suhayl, one of Mālik's main shaykhs; see below), from Abū Hurayra.

12. Rabīʿa ibn ʿAbd al-Raḥmān (d. between 130/747 and 136/753)

Rabīʿa – known as 'Rabīʿat al-Raʾy', or 'Rabīʿa of the Informed Opinion' – was one of the first, if not the first, of Mālik's main teachers. We are told that Mālik's mother took the decision to set Mālik on a path of study and, after dressing him up in 'the clothes of learning', told him to go to Rabīʿa to study, advising him to learn from his behaviour before his knowledge.[45]

Mālik had a particularly high opinion of Rabīʿa: when Rabīʿa died, he commented that the sweetness of *fiqh* had gone.[46]

Mālik relates twelve Prophetic *ḥadīth*s from Rabīʿa in the *Muwaṭṭaʾ*. These are from various sources, including, from among the Seven/Ten Jurists, one from al-Qāsim ibn Muḥammad and one from Sulaymān ibn Yasār.

13. Suhayl ibn Abī Ṣāliḥ al-Sammān (d. beginning of caliphate of Abū Jaʿfar al-Manṣūr (r. 136–58/754–75))

Suhayl's father, Abū Ṣāliḥ al-Sammān (d. 101/719), was the *mawlā* of a woman called Juwayriya of the Ghaṭafān tribe. Abū Ṣāliḥ was a key source of *ḥadīth* for many of the scholars of the people of Medina of the generation before Mālik – including, as we have seen, Sumayy, the *mawlā* of Abū Bakr – and, in particular, of the *ḥadīths* transmitted by Abū Hurayra, who said of him, by way of praise, 'This man has been done no harm by not being one of the descendants of ʿAbd Manāf!' – in other words, in having slave origins rather than being one of the tribe of Quraysh.[47]

Mālik relates ten *musnad ḥadīths* from Suhayl ibn Abī Ṣāliḥ in the *Muwaṭṭa*ʾ, all of which are from his father, Abū Ṣāliḥ, from Abū Hurayra, from the Prophet.

14. ʿAbd al-Raḥmān ibn al-Qāsim (d. *c.* 126/743)

ʿAbd al-Raḥmān ibn al-Qāsim was the son of al-Qāsim ibn Muḥammad ibn Abī Bakr, one of the Seven/Ten Jurists of Medina. ʿAbd al-Raḥmān's mother was Qurayba, the daughter of ʿAbd al-Raḥmān ibn Abī Bakr. ʿAbd al-Raḥmān was thus the great-grandson of the first caliph Abū Bakr through both his father and his mother.

An anecdote is told of how Mālik's son, Yaḥyā, was entering and leaving the room where his father was teaching and would not sit down and participate. Mālik noticed him and said, 'What makes this situation easier for me is that this business cannot be inherited. No-one has taken the place of his father except for ʿAbd al-Raḥmān ibn al-Qāsim ibn Muḥammad ibn Abī Bakr al-Ṣiddīq – may Allah be pleased with him. He was the best man of his time, and his father was the best man of *his* time.'[48]

Mālik includes ten Prophetic *ḥadīths* from ʿAbd al-Raḥmān ibn al-Qāsim in the *Muwaṭṭa*ʾ, eight of which are via his father, al-Qāsim, six of them in turn from al-Qāsim's aunt, ʿĀʾisha. (Of the other two, one is without a full *isnād*, and the other is from ʿAbdallāh, the son of ʿAbdallāh ibn ʿUmar.)

15. Al-ʿAlāʾ ibn ʿAbd al-Raḥmān (d. 139/756)

Al-ʿAlāʾ ibn ʿAbd al-Raḥmān ibn Yaʿqūb, 'the *mawlā* of the Ḥuraqa', was one of the Younger Successors; his father was also a Successor, and his grandfather was one of the Older Successors. Yaʿqūb was a *mukātab* slave belonging to Aws ibn al-Ḥadathān al-Naṣrī and he married a slave girl belonging to a man of the Ḥuraqa tribe. She gave birth to ʿAbd al-Raḥmān, but, because she did so before Yaʿqūb had paid off his *kitāba*, the *walāʾ* of her son was judged by ʿUthmān to go to *her* former owner, not his, hence the *nisba* of 'the *mawlā* of the Ḥuraqa'.[49]

Mālik relates nine *musnad ḥadīths* from al-ʿAlāʾ ibn ʿAbd al-Raḥmān in the *Muwaṭṭaʾ*, but Ibn ʿAbd al-Barr includes a tenth *ḥadīth* which, he says, must be Prophetic, because of its meaning and because of the existence of full *isnāds* for it elsewhere, although Mālik himself says of it, 'I don't know whether he attributes this to the Prophet, may Allah bless him and grant him peace, or not.'[50] Five of these ten *ḥadīths* are via his father, ʿAbd al-Raḥmān. An eleventh report is included in the *Muwaṭṭaʾ* on the authority of al-ʿAlāʾ, from his father, from his grandfather, about ʿUthmān.

* * * * *

The above fifteen are the teachers of Mālik from whom he relates ten or more Prophetic *ḥadīths* in the *Muwaṭṭaʾ*. He had, of course, many other teachers, some of whom we mention here because of their particular interest.

16. Jaʿfar ibn Muḥammad (d. 148/765)

Jaʿfar ibn Muḥammad ibn ʿAlī ibn al-Ḥusayn ibn ʿAlī ibn Abī Ṭālib was a great-great-grandson of the fourth caliph, ʿAlī ibn Abī Ṭālib, and, in that capacity, is considered the Sixth Imam of the Twelver Shiʿas (following on from his father Muḥammad, his grandfather ʿAlī ibn al-Ḥusayn, his great-grandfather al-Ḥusayn, his great-great-uncle al-Ḥasan and his great-great-grandfather ʿAlī). Jaʿfar's mother was Farwa, the daughter of al-Qāsim ibn Muḥammad ibn Abī Bakr (as noted above, one of the Seven/Ten Jurists and the father of Mālik's shaykh ʿAbd al-Raḥmān ibn al-Qāsim). Jaʿfar was thus not only a direct descendant of the fourth caliph ʿAlī but also of the first caliph Abū Bakr – which should alert us to the intellectually questionable nature of some groups revering the one and reviling the other.

Mālik said of him,

> I often used to visit Jaʿfar ibn Muḥammad and I would always find him busy in one of three things: either he would be doing the prayer, or fasting, or reciting the Qur'an. I only ever saw him relate *ḥadīths* from the Messenger of Allah,

> may Allah bless him and grant him peace, if he was in *wuḍū'* (state of 'minor' ablution) and he would never speak about what did not concern him. He was one of the men of knowledge who were known for their devotion, their doing without the things of this world, and their fear of Allah. One year I went on *ḥajj* with him. When he came to al-Shajara he went into *iḥrām*, but, every time he tried to declare his intention to begin [his *ḥajj*], he would be overcome. I said to him, 'You have to do it.' He was kind and well-disposed towards me, and said, 'Son of Ibn 'Āmir, I am afraid if I say *Labbayk, Allāhumma labbayk* ('I am at your service, Allah, I am at Your service'), He will say, *Lā labbayk, wa-lā sa'dayk* ('You are not at My service, nor are you welcome').'

Mālik added, 'Once his grandfather, 'Alī ibn al-Ḥusayn, went into *iḥrām* and, when he wanted to say – or said – *Labbayk, Allāhumma, labbayk*, he went into a swoon, fell off his camel and hurt his face.'[51]

Mālik relates nine Prophetic *ḥadīth*s from Ja'far ibn Muḥammad in the *Muwaṭṭa'* (although, according to Ibn 'Abd al-Barr, five of them derive from one longer *ḥadīth* from the Companion Jābir about *ḥajj*).[52] All of these *ḥadīth*s are related by Ja'far from his father Muḥammad.

17. Nāfi' ibn Mālik, Abū Suhayl (d. between 132/750 and 136/754)

Abū Suhayl was Mālik's uncle. The *Muwaṭṭa'* includes two Prophetic *ḥadīth*s from him, both of which are related in turn from his father (Mālik's grandfather), Mālik ibn Abī 'Āmir. The *Muwaṭṭa'* also includes nine other reports from Abū Suhayl, eight of which are from his father. There are also two further reports that Mālik relates on the authority of his grandfather, one a Prophetic *ḥadīth* and the other about 'Uthmān.

18. Muḥammad ibn al-Munkadir ibn al-Ḥuḍayr (d. 130/747 or 131/748)

As well as having an extensive knowledge of *fiqh*, Ibn al-Munkadir was renowned in Medina as a man of high spiritual status whose prayers were answered, and who was very generous, despite not being well off. His mother was a slave-girl.

The strong impression that he made on Mālik is evident in Mālik's words about him: 'Muhammad ibn al-Munkadir was a lord among Qur'an reciters, and would weep a lot when [teaching] *ḥadīth*. If I found myself feeling hard-hearted in any way, I would go to him, look at him and be reminded by him, and the benefit would last for days. He used to pray a lot at night.'[53]

Mālik relates five Prophetic *ḥadīth*s from him in the *Muwaṭṭa*ʾ (along with three other reports: two from ʿUmar and one on his own authority).

19. ʿAbdallāh ibn ʿAbd al-Raḥmān ibn Maʿmar, Abū Ṭuwāla (d. at the end of the Umayyad caliphate i.e. *c.* 130/747)

Abū Ṭuwāla was the judge of Medina during Abū Bakr ibn Ḥazm's governorate. Mālik said of him,

> ʿAbdallāh ibn ʿAbd al-Raḥmān ibn Maʿmar was a man of excellent behaviour (*rajul ṣāliḥ*). He was a judge during the caliphates of Sulaymān [r. 96–9/715–17] and ʿUmar ibn ʿAbd al-ʿAzīz [r. 99–101/717–20]. He would fast a lot. He was able to express himself very well. He would go in to see the governor and advise him and tell him where the truth lay in any situation without trying to make things easy for him, whereas other people would be afraid of being beaten.[54]

Among the sayings recorded from Abū Ṭuwāla is the following: 'If only we had the behaviour of our forefathers in the Jāhiliyya along with our Islam!'[55]

Mālik relates three Prophetic *ḥadīth*s from Abū Ṭuwāla in the *Muwaṭṭa*ʾ.

20. ʿAbd al-Raḥmān ibn Ḥarmala al-Aslamī, Abū Ḥarmala (d. in the caliphate of Abū l-ʿAbbās al-Saffāḥ (r. 132–6/749–54) or in 145/762)

ʿAbd al-Raḥmān's father, Ḥarmala, was a Companion and, like his son, was also a transmitter of *ḥadīth*. However, the reason for mentioning ʿAbd al-Raḥmān here is that there are two rock inscriptions in the Ḥismā region of north-western Saudi Arabia that bear his name and thus provide documentary evidence of his existence. The first inscription, at Shaʿib al-Hashūsh (?), reads, 'I am Abū Ḥarmala, ʿAbd al-Raḥmān ibn Ḥarmala al-Aslamī. I advise [people] to have fear of Allah, the Great.' The second, in the vicinity of Tabuk, reads, 'I am ʿAbd al-Raḥmān ibn Ḥarmala al-Aslamī. I ask Allah for the Garden as a final resort, for His pleasure as a reward, and for the believers as companions. Amin, Lord of the Worlds.'[56]

Mālik relates five Prophetic *ḥadīth*s from ʿAbd al-Raḥmān ibn Ḥarmala in the *Muwaṭṭaʾ*.[57]

* * * * *

We noted earlier that Ibn ʿAbd al-Barr mentions a total of ninety-eight shaykhs from whom Mālik transmits *ḥadīth* from the Prophet in the *Muwaṭṭaʾ*. There are also, however, shaykhs from whom he transmits only non-Prophetic material and which Ibn ʿAbd al-Barr thus does not include in his *Tamhīd*. Among these, the following three may be noted as examples:

21. Saʿīd ibn Sulaymān ibn Zayd ibn Thābit (d. 132/742)

We referred above to Mālik transmitting a report from Khārija (from his father Zayd ibn Thābit), one of the Seven/Ten Jurists of Medina, via his nephew Saʿīd ibn Sulaymān ibn Zayd ibn Thābit. Saʿīd was at one time judge of Medina (during the caliphate of Hishām ibn ʿAbd al-Malik (r. 105–25/724–43)). Mālik said of him,

> When Saʿīd ibn Sulaymān ibn Zayd ibn Thābit was appointed [judge], he didn't want to take it on and asked the governor of Medina to excuse him. The governor gathered together the shaykhs of the people of Medina – and Saʿīd was someone who was very diligent in doing the prayer – [these shaykhs including] Saʿd ibn Ibrāhīm [the judge before him], Abū Salama ibn ʿAbd al-Raḥmān [judge in the time of Muʿāwiya, and one of the Seven/Ten Jurists of Medina], Muḥammad ibn Muṣʿab ibn [Abī] Ḥanbal and Muḥammad ibn Ṣafwān, and they all said to him, 'To judge by the truth for one day (*qaḍāʾ yawm bi-l-ḥaqq*) is better in our opinion than doing the prayer for the whole of your life', at which point he accepted being a judge.[58]

22. Abū Jaʿfar Yazīd ibn al-Qaʿqāʿ (d. *c.* 130/747)

Abū Jaʿfar was the chief Qur'an reciter in Medina in his day, having taught the Qur'an in Medina since before the Battle of al-Ḥarra (63/683), and his reading is one of the Ten Readings commonly recognized by the Muslims. Mālik relates four Companion reports from Abū Jaʿfar in the *Muwaṭṭaʾ*, three of them about ʿAbdallāh ibn ʿUmar and one about ʿAbdallāh ibn ʿAyyāsh.

23. ʿUrwa ibn Udhayna

We should also bear in mind that Mālik did not only relate from scholars and specialists of *ḥadīth*. There is, for example, a report in the *Muwaṭṭaʾ* (which is also recorded in the *Mudawwana*) from the well-respected Medinan poet, ʿUrwa ibn Udhayna – who was a friend of Hishām ibn ʿAbd al-Malik before Hishām became caliph and left Medina for Damascus – about an incident concerning his grandmother when both of them were on the way to Mecca for *ḥajj* or *ʿumra*. She had vowed to walk to Mecca but then, while on her way, became unable to do so. She asked a *mawlā* of hers to ask ʿAbdallāh ibn ʿUmar what she should do, and ʿUrwa went with him. (ʿAbdallāh ibn ʿUmar said she should ride to Mecca and then fulfil her oath by walking, from the place where she had stopped, in a future year.)[59] Many centuries later, this one report was to cause exaggerated criticism of Mālik by the Hungarian scholar Goldziher (see further Chapter 5).

24. ʿAbdallāh ibn Yazīd ibn Hurmuz (d. 148/765)

Last, but not least, we should mention one of Mālik's first and most influential teachers, the younger Medinan Successor ʿAbdallāh ibn Yazīd ibn Hurmuz, who is also one of the least known. It is said that Mālik studied solely under Ibn Hurmuz for a period of at least seven years, although one report suggests that the total time he spent with him was more like thirty years.[60] Despite this long time – and in contrast to his other main teachers such as Ibn Shihāb and Nāfiʿ – Ibn Hurmuz is only rarely cited as an authority – and never in the *Muwaṭṭaʾ* – and, when he is cited, it is never as a transmitter of *ḥadīth*. The sources explain that this was because he had made Mālik swear that he would never transmit a *ḥadīth* from him mentioning his name.[61]

Sometimes we find Ibn Hurmuz's name mentioned alongside that of Rabīʿa, and it seems clear that the two were closely associated. Thus, out of nine references to Ibn Hurmuz in the *Mudawwana*, three of them include mention of Rabīʿa;[62] and, out of twenty-one in the *ʿUtbiyya*, five also contain mention of Rabīʿa.[63] It is said that, when Mālik uses phrases such as 'This is what I found the people of our city doing', 'the people of knowledge in our city' or 'the matter which we are all agreed upon here', it is Rabīʿa and Ibn Hurmuz that he is referring to.[64]

* * * * *

These, then, are some of the teachers from whom Mālik transmitted his knowledge. They include people whose main task was to transmit this material to others, and others whose main task was to dispense justice in a formal sense, as judges, in accordance with this knowledge; but they also include, as with ʿUrwa ibn Udhayna, people who were simply living in Medina as Muslims. In many instances, they include, as we have seen, people who were direct descendants of some of the most important Companions, including the first four Rightly Guided Caliphs. In all instances, they were people who shared this common heritage of the city and were concerned to keep it alive and pass it on to future generations, both in word and deed.

Transmission by word leads us to a consideration of the written word and 'books', which in Mālik's case means primarily his *Muwaṭṭaʾ*, which is the subject of Chapter 3. Transmission by deed leads us to a consideration of the *ʿamal*, or 'practice', of the people of Medina, which is the subject of Chapter 4.

3

The *Muwaṭṭa*ʾ

A number of writings are attributed to Mālik, and sayings and opinions of his are recorded in various other sources, but by far his most important work is the *Muwaṭṭa*ʾ. The *Muwaṭṭa*ʾ is particularly interesting not only because of the high standing of its author – or perhaps we should say its compiler, as most of the material in it is transmitted, as we have seen, from earlier authorities – and the reliability of his material but also because of its historical precedence: it is, in effect, our first compendium of Islamic law and our first book of *ḥadīth* organized according to subject matter. (There are fragments of other early legal works that exist,[1] but the *Muwaṭṭa*ʾ is characterized by its completeness and its multiple transmissions.)

As to the excellence of its author, we have already referred earlier (see Chapter 1) to the well-known *ḥadīth* that 'the time is nigh when people will beat the livers of their camels [i.e. urge them on] in search of knowledge, but they will not find anyone more knowledgeable than the scholar of Medina', and we saw that this was taken to refer to Imam Mālik. As a contemporary of his, Ibn ʿUyayna, put it,

> I used to say that it was [Saʿīd] ibn al-Musayyab, but then I said [to myself] that in the time of Ibn al-Musayyab there were also Sulaymān [ibn Yasār], Sālim [ibn ʿAbdallāh ibn ʿUmar] and others [in Medina]. Now I say that it was Mālik, because he lived until a time when there was no one else left in Medina that was equal to him.[2]

Mālik's excellence with regard to *ḥadīth* scholarship was acknowledged by his contemporaries, and it earned him the title of *amīr al-muʾminīn fī l-ḥadīth* – 'the commander of the faithful with regard to *ḥadīth*'.[3] He was described by Aḥmad ibn Ḥanbal, the fourth of the imams of the Four Madhhabs, as 'an imam in *ḥadīth* and *fiqh*'.[4] The famous *ḥadīth* scholar and transmitter of the

*Muwaṭṭa*ʾ, Ibn Mahdī, put the same idea in the following terms: 'Al-Thawrī is an imam with regard to *ḥadīth* but not an imam with regard to the *sunna*; al-Awzāʿī is an imam with regard to the *sunna*, but not an imam with regard to *ḥadīth*. Mālik, however, is an imam with regard to both.'[5]

As for authenticity of the *Muwaṭṭa*ʾ, it was the view of Imam al-Shāfiʿī, one of Mālik's main students and the founder of the third of the Four Madhhabs, that 'there is no book on earth, after the Qur'an, which is more accurate (*aṣaḥḥ*) than the book of Mālik',[6] while the scholar Abū Zurʿa said, 'If someone were to make an oath on pain of divorce that all the *ḥadīth*s in the *Muwaṭṭa*ʾ were sound, he would not have to expiate his oath, whereas if he were to say the same about anyone else's *ḥadīth*s, he would have to do so.'[7]

As for its historical precedence, we restrict ourselves to the comments of three prominent scholars:

1. The Mālikī scholar Qadi Abū Bakr ibn al-ʿArabī (d. 543/1148) says, in his commentary on the *Ṣaḥīḥ* of al-Tirmidhī, 'The *Muwaṭṭa*ʾ is the first source and the core, while the book of al-Bukhārī is the second source in this respect; the rest, such as Muslim and al-Tirmidhī, built on the basis of these two.'[8]
2. The Ḥanafī *ḥadīth* scholar al-Ḥāfiẓ Mughalṭāy (d. 762/1361) said that Mālik was the first to organize authentic *ḥadīth* into content-based chapters (*awwal man ṣannafa al-ṣaḥīḥ*).[9]
3. In his *Ḥujjat Allāh al-Bāligha*, the highly respected scholar Shāh Walī Allāh al-Dihlawī (1114–1176/1704–1762) confirms the primacy of Mālik's *Muwaṭṭa*ʾ, followed by the two *Ṣaḥīḥ* collections of al-Bukhārī and Muslim.[10]

The different transmissions of the *Muwaṭṭa*ʾ

As was the nature of texts recorded in Mālik's time, the *Muwaṭṭa*ʾ has come down to us in the form of various transmissions (*riwāyāt*). These differ from one another to a greater or lesser degree in terms of details in the wording of the texts, the wording of the different chapter headings, the order of these chapters and, in some cases, the inclusion or exclusion of larger portions of material. Nevertheless, these different transmissions share an overwhelming overall similarity, which enables us to have a high degree of certainty about their attribution to one and the same source, and one and the same place, namely, Mālik in Medina.

Over ninety people are on record as having transmitted the *Muwaṭṭa᾿* directly from Mālik, but, despite this number, far fewer transmissions have actually survived to this day in published or manuscript form. To the best of my knowledge, there are eight transmissions of the text that are currently available in printed and/or manuscript form. Four of these are complete, while the other four are incomplete to differing degrees. These eight printed versions are those of the following:

1. Yaḥyā ibn Yaḥyā al-Laythī (complete)
2. Abū Muṣ῾ab al-Zuhrī (complete)
3. Al-Shaybānī (complete)
4. Yaḥyā ibn Bukayr (complete; a few folios already published)
5. Suwayd al-Ḥadathānī (incomplete, but extensive)
6. Al-Qa῾nabī (incomplete; only a few chapters)
7. ῾Alī ibn Ziyād (incomplete; only a few chapters)
8. Ibn al-Qāsim (incomplete, but most *musnad ḥadīth*s included)

We shall look briefly at each in turn.

1. Yaḥyā ibn Yaḥyā al-Laythī (d. 234/848; from al-Andalus). Yaḥyā first transmitted the *Muwaṭṭa᾿* in his native Andalus from the Andalusian scholar Ziyād ibn Shabṭūn ῾Abd al-Raḥmān (known as 'Shabṭūn'), who had transmitted it from the Tunisian scholar ῾Alī ibn Ziyād (for whom, see further below). Yaḥyā then travelled to Medina and transmitted the whole of the text directly from Mālik, apart from a very short portion consisting of four out of six chapters of the Book of *I῾tikāf* which still retain their immediate attribution to Ziyād (ibn ῾Abd al-Raḥmān) rather than Mālik.[11] Yaḥyā's journey to Medina took place in the year 179/795, in the last year of Mālik's life, and his transmission thus represents a late – although probably not the latest – version of the text (see further below, under Abū Muṣ῾ab). Mālik recognized Yaḥyā's qualities and referred to him as 'the intelligent one (*῾āqil*) of al-Andalus'.[12]

Yaḥyā's transmission has been published many times, in many editions, as have numerous commentaries on it.

2. Muḥammad ibn al-Ḥasan al-Shaybānī (d. 189/805; from Kufa, but later settled in Baghdad). Al-Shaybānī was one of the main students of Abū Ḥanīfa and was effectively responsible, along with Abū Ḥanīfa's other main student Abū Yūsuf, for transmitting the learning of the Iraqi city of Kufa that later became the Ḥanafī *madhhab*. Al-Shaybānī spent three years studying under Mālik[13] and transmitted a version of the *Muwaṭṭaʾ* from him. His transmission is significantly different in form: while it retains much of the material common to the other transmissions, it at times includes and at times omits a certain number of Prophetic *ḥadīth*s found in other versions, and the order that the material is presented in is different. His transmission is also characterized by the exclusion of the opinions of Mālik and the Medinans, preferring instead to highlight the views of Abū Ḥanīfa and the Kufans. Al-Shaybānī's transmission has been published a number of times, as have various commentaries on it.

3. Abū Muṣʿab al-Zuhrī (d. 242/856; from Medina). Abū Muṣʿab Aḥmad ibn Abī Bakr al-Qāsim ibn al-Ḥārith ibn Zurāra ibn Muṣʿab ibn ʿAbd al-Raḥmān ibn ʿAwf, to give him his full name, was the great-great-great-grandson of the Companion ʿAbd al-Raḥmān ibn ʿAwf. (We have already noted two men of knowledge connected with ʿAbd al-Raḥmān's family: first, his son Abū Salama, one of the Seven Jurists of Medina; and second, Mālik's shaykh Ṣafwān ibn Sulaym, whose father Sulaym was the *mawlā* of ʿAbd al-Raḥmān's son Ḥumayd ibn ʿAbd al-Raḥmān ibn ʿAwf.) Abū Muṣʿab was born in Medina and, like Mālik, lived there for the whole of his life. In his later years he became judge of the city.

A complete edition of Abū Muṣʿab's transmission, from a unique manuscript in the Salar Jang Library in Hyderabad, India – although fragments of this transmission exist in other libraries – has been edited and published. Abū Muṣʿab's transmission is very similar to that of Yaḥyā ibn Yaḥyā, although in general it is a little longer. The Andalusian scholar Ibn Ḥazm, generalizing, said that it contains 'about 100 *ḥadīth*s' more than Yaḥyā's transmission,[14] while the editor of the printed text specifies that it contains twenty-four Prophetic *ḥadīth*s which either do not occur in Yaḥyā's transmission or occur in it without a full *isnād*, but ten other *ḥadīth*s that occur in a 'fuller' version in Abū Muṣʿab's transmission, as well as thirty-two extra Companion reports, seventeen extra Successor reports and sixty-eight extra opinions of Mālik not contained in

Yaḥyā's transmission.[15] There are also minor differences in chapter order and in some details of the wording. It is considered – along with the transmission of Abū Ḥudhāfa al-Sahmī, which contains a roughly similar number of extra *ḥadīth*s – to be the latest of the transmissions of the *Muwaṭṭaʾ*.[16]

4. Yaḥyā ibn Bukayr (d. 231/845; from Egypt). His full name is Yaḥyā ibn ʿAbdallāh ibn Bukayr, but he is usually known simply as Yaḥyā ibn Bukayr, or just Ibn Bukayr. He is said to have gone through the *Muwaṭṭaʾ* seventeen times with Mālik (one at least of which would have been towards the end of Mālik's life, as Ibn Bukayr is said to have travelled to see Mālik in the year 178/794). His transmission is one of five referred to by Ibn ʿAbd al-Barr in his commentary on the *Muwaṭṭaʾ*, the *Istidhkār*. (The other four are the transmissions of Yaḥyā ibn Yaḥyā al-Laythī, Ibn al-Qāsim, al-Qaʿnabī and Muṭarrif.)[17] An edition of Ibn Bukayr's transmission was published in Algiers in 1905, and manuscript copies exist in the Ẓāhiriyya Library in Damascus, the Suleymaniye Library in Istanbul, the National Library in Algiers and in various collections in Morocco.[18] In terms of its form, it is very similar to the transmission of Yaḥyā ibn Yaḥyā al-Laythī (although the North African manuscripts seem characterized by incomplete *isnād*s which only mention the name of the last major authority).[19]

5. Suwayd al-Ḥadathānī (d. 240/854; from al-Ḥadītha, in Iraq). An incomplete, but extensive, fragment of the transmission of Suwayd al-Ḥadathānī exists in the Ẓāhiriyya Library in Damascus and has been edited and published.

6. al-Qaʿnabī (d. 220/835; from Medina; settled in Basra but died in Mecca). His full name is ʿAbdallāh ibn Maslama ibn Qaʿnab. Al-Qaʿnabī is considered by many – along with ʿAbdallāh ibn Yūsuf al-Tinnīsī – to be the most reliable transmitter of the *Muwaṭṭaʾ*. His transmission was the one preferred by Abū Dāwūd (among the compilers of the Six Books of *ḥadīth*). It is also said to be the one with the most additional material in it (*akbarihā*).[20] Al-Qaʿnabī spent twenty years studying the *Muwaṭṭaʾ* under Mālik and was once praised by him as being 'the best of people on the earth'.[21]

Portions of this transmission in a unique manuscript in the National Library in Tunis have been edited and published.[22]

7. ʿAlī ibn Ziyād al-Tūnisī (d. 183/799; from Tunis). A unique manuscript preserved in Qayrawan which contains a small portion of ʿAlī ibn Ziyād's transmission has been edited and published. His transmission is considerably earlier than that of Yaḥyā ibn Yaḥyā al-Laythī and can be dated to around the year 150 AH.

8. ʿAbd al-Raḥmān ibn al-Qāsim (d. 191/806; from Egypt). Fragments of Ibn al-Qāsim's transmission exist in manuscript form in Tunis and Qayrawan, and elsewhere.[23] In his *Mulakhkhaṣ*, al-Qābisī (324–403/936–1012) collected together the *ḥadīth*s of this transmission that have a full *isnād*, and this work of al-Qābisī has been published as 'the *Muwaṭṭaʾ* in the transmission of Ibn al-Qāsim'.

Ibn al-Qāsim was one of the main students of Mālik and, like al-Qaʿnabī, spent twenty years studying under Mālik.[24] In addition to transmitting the *Muwaṭṭaʾ*, Ibn al-Qāsim was also responsible for transmitting the opinions and judgements of Mālik that now constitute the major Mālikī text known as the *Mudawwana*.[25]

9. ʿAbdallāh ibn Wahb (d. 197/812; from Egypt). Mention should also be made of the transmission of Ibn Wahb, traces of which are found throughout the *ḥadīth* literature in the form of Ibn Wahb's direct transmissions from Mālik.[26] A book published recently with the title 'the *Muwaṭṭaʾ* of Ibn Wahb' is clearly not a transmission of Mālik's *Muwaṭṭaʾ* – there is very little mention of Mālik in it – but rather Ibn Wahb's own '*Muwaṭṭaʾ*'.[27] Ibn Wahb features regularly as an authority in the *Mudawwana*.

There is, however, one other route of transmission that has been noted by scholars but often overlooked. This is the transmission of the same material from Mālik – and thus effectively of his *Muwaṭṭaʾ* – in the later collections of *ḥadīth*. If we consider the Six Books, for example, that is, the collections of al-Bukhārī, Muslim, Abū Dāwūd, al-Tirmidhī, al-Nasāʾī and Ibn Mājah, we find that they often rely on specific transmissions from Mālik different from the published ones noted above. Thus, for example, al-Bukhārī, in his *Ṣaḥīḥ*, relies extensively on the transmission of ʿAbdallāh ibn Yūsuf al-Tinnīsī, although also on the transmissions of Maʿn ibn ʿĪsā and al-Qaʿnabī; Muslim, in his *Ṣaḥīḥ*, relies mostly on the transmission of Yaḥyā ibn Yaḥyā al-Tamīmī al-Naysābūrī

(d. 226/840) (not to be confused with Yaḥyā ibn Yaḥyā al-Laythī); Abū Dāwūd, in his *Sunan*, relies mostly, as we have mentioned, on the transmission of al-Qaʿnabī; al-Tirmidhī often relates directly from Qutayba ibn Saʿīd (d. 240/854), from Mālik, but also indirectly via Maʿn ibn ʿĪsā; while al-Nasāʾī is said to have preferred the transmission of al-Qaʿnabī and/or relied on that of Qutayba ibn Saʿīd. Ibn Mājah, being somewhat later than the others, only relates small numbers of *ḥadīth*s from people who transmitted directly from Mālik, but, of those people, the names of Suwayd ibn Saʿīd [al-Ḥadathānī] and Hishām ibn ʿAmmār stand out. To this list can be added the *Musnad* of Imam Aḥmad ibn Ḥanbal, who relies particularly on the transmission of ʿAbd al-Raḥmān ibn Mahdī; and the collections of Ibn al-Madīnī, who, like Abū Dāwūd and al-Nasāʾī, relied mostly on the transmission of al-Qaʿnabī, and of Abū Ḥātim, who relied mostly on the transmission of Maʿn ibn ʿĪsā.[28] It can thus be seen that, in this sense, the Six Books and the other collections of *ḥadīth* mentioned effectively preserve other transmissions of the *Muwaṭṭaʾ*. The same applies to al-Shāfiʿī, whose *Kitāb al-Umm*, as pointed out recently by Ahmed El Shamsy, effectively contains portions of his own transmission of the *Muwaṭṭaʾ*.[29] (See further below.)

It is clear from the above that we have many transmissions of this text, the *Muwaṭṭaʾ*, making for a highly reliable text. But what are the differences, if any, between these different transmissions?

The differences between the transmissions

Some transmissions, such as that of al-Shaybānī, appear significantly different from that of Yaḥyā ibn Yaḥyā al-Laythī, while others are remarkably similar. An idea of the differences – and similarities – between these transmissions can be gained by a comparison of some key chapters between the various transmissions available (namely, in the present instance, those of Yaḥyā ibn Yaḥyā al-Laythī, Abū Muṣʿab al-Zuhrī, Ibn Bukayr, al-Qaʿnabī, Suwayd and al-Shaybānī). Two examples – dictated by the illustrations available in printed form of a manuscript of Ibn Bukayr's transmission – will suffice, the first from the Book of *Zakāt*, and the second from the Book of Fasting.

Example 1: From the Book of *Zakāt*

In the transmission of Yaḥyā ibn Yaḥyā al-Laythī, the Book of *Zakāt* begins with a chapter entitled 'What *Zakāt* Is Due On'. This chapter contains four reports: two Prophetic *ḥadīth*s of very similar import followed by a report from the 'Fifth Rightly-Guided Caliph', ʿUmar ibn ʿAbd al-ʿAzīz, and then a brief comment by Mālik, as follows:

> 1. Yaḥyā related to me from Mālik, from ʿAmr ibn Yaḥyā al-Māzinī, that his father said: 'I heard Abū Saʿīd al-Khudrī say, that the Messenger of Allah, may Allah bless him and grant him peace, said: "There is no *zakāt* on less than five camels; there is no *zakāt* on less than five *ūqiyya*s [of silver]; and there is no *zakāt* on less than five *wasq*s." ' [An *ūqiyya* is a weight, equivalent to forty dirhams. A dirham weighs approx. 2.97 g, so an *ūqiyya* weighs approx. 40 × 2.97 = 119 g. A *wasq* is a measure, not a weight, but is roughly equivalent to 128 kg.][30]
>
> 2. Yaḥyā related to me from Mālik, from Muḥammad ibn ʿAbdallāh ibn ʿAbd al-Raḥmān ibn Abī Ṣaʿṣaʿa al-Anṣārī, later al-Māzinī, from his father, from Abū Saʿīd al-Khudrī, that the Messenger of Allah, may Allah bless him and grant him peace, said: 'There is no *zakāt* on less than five *wasq*s of dates; there is no *zakāt* on less than five *ūqiyya*s of silver; and there is no *zakāt* on less than five camels.'
>
> 3. Yaḥyā related to me from Mālik that he had heard that ʿUmar ibn ʿAbd al-ʿAzīz had written to his governor in Damascus about *zakāt*, saying: '*Zakāt* only applies to crops, gold and silver, and livestock.'
>
> 4. Mālik said: '*Zakāt* only applies to three things: crops, gold and silver, and livestock.'[31]

The transmission of al-Zuhrī contains the same reports, and in the same order, although there are some minor differences in detail. In the second report, the immediate source of Mālik is given as ʿ**Abd al-Raḥmān** ibn ʿAbdallāh ibn ʿAbd al-Raḥmān, rather than Muḥammad, and his *nisba* is given simply as 'al-Māzinī', without mentioning 'al-Anṣārī'. In the third and fourth reports, the three categories are given in a slightly different order: where Yaḥyā has 'crops-coin-camels', al-Zuhrī has 'coin-crops-livestock'.[32]

If we look at Ibn Bukayr's transmission (as represented by the two published folios from the Ẓāhiriyya manuscript), we find the same four reports, in the same order, but again with minor differences. The first *ḥadīth* is the same, except that the grammatical gender of the word 'five' is different. In the second *ḥadīth*, Mālik's source is given as '**Abd al-Raḥmān** ibn 'Abdallāh ibn 'Abd al-Raḥmān, and his *nisba* is also given simply as 'al-Māzinī', as in al-Zuhrī's transmission; the order of the categories is also different, with silver and camels put before dates, and the phrase 'of silver' is not included. In the third and fourth reports, the order is the same as with al-Zuhrī, although Ibn Bukayr's transmission also includes a short report (after No. 3 above about 'Umar ibn 'Abd al-'Azīz) from Ibn Shihāb to the effect that Sulaymān ibn Yasār said that there is no *zakāt* on less than five *ūqiyyas*.[33]

The published fragment of Suwayd's transmission includes a general section on *zakāt*, but the whole section is much shorter than the Book of *Zakāt* in the transmissions of Yaḥyā and al-Zuhrī, and consists simply of fourteen reports under the general heading of 'What has come down about *zakāt*'. However, it does contain the first two Prophetic *ḥadīth*s mentioned in the other three transmissions. They have exactly the same content, except that Mālik's direct source for the second is given as **Muḥammad** ibn 'Abdallāh ibn 'Abd al-Raḥmān ibn Abī Ṣa'ṣa'a (as in Yaḥyā's transmission), and he does not mention either 'al-Anṣārī' or 'al-Māzinī'.[34]

Al-Shaybānī's transmission is rather different. He includes only the second of the two Prophetic *ḥadīth*s – with the same content as the other transmissions, but citing, as in Yaḥyā's and Suwayd's transmissions, **Muḥammad** ibn 'Abdallāh ibn 'Abd al-Raḥmān ibn Abī Ṣa'ṣa'a as Mālik's source (and without mentioning either 'al-Anṣārī' or 'al-Māzinī', as with Suwayd). Al-Shaybānī does not include the report about 'Umar ibn 'Abd al-'Azīz (No. 3), nor the comment from Mālik (No. 4). Instead, he includes a comment about Abū Ḥanīfa's view, saying,

> This is what we go by, and what Abū Ḥanīfa used to go by, except in one situation, namely, that a tenth should be taken from what the earth produces, whether it is a little or a lot, if it has been irrigated by naturally flowing water or rain from the sky; if, however, it has been irrigated using a bucket or a water-wheel, only a twentieth is due. This was [also] the opinion of Ibrāhīm al-Nakha'ī and Mujāhid.[35]

In Yaḥyā's transmission, the above chapter is followed by a chapter entitled '*Zakāt* on Gold and Silver'. This consists of four *ḥadīth* reports, followed by nine reports from Mālik, as follows:

1. Yaḥyā related to me, from Mālik, that Muḥammad ibn ʿUqba, the *mawlā* of al-Zubayr, asked al-Qāsim ibn Muḥammad about a *mukātab* slave of his from whom he had received, by arrangement, a large sum of money (*qāṭaʿahu bi-mālin ʿaẓīm*) [i.e. in order to speed up his manumission], and whether he should pay *zakāt* on it. Al-Qāsim said: 'Abū Bakr al-Ṣiddīq would not take *zakāt* from anybody's money until that person had had it for a year.' Al-Qāsim ibn Muḥammad added: 'When Abū Bakr gave people their stipends, he would ask each person whether he had any money on which he needed to pay *zakāt*. If he said "Yes", he would take the *zakāt* due on that money out of his stipend, and if he said "No", he would give him his stipend and not take anything from it.'

2. [Yaḥyā] related to me, from ʿUmar ibn Ḥusayn, from ʿĀʾisha bint Qudāma, that her father said: 'Whenever I came to ʿUthmān ibn ʿAffān to receive my stipend, he would ask me whether I had any money on which I needed to pay *zakāt*. If I said "Yes", he would take the *zakāt* due on that money from my stipend, and if I said "No", he would give me my stipend.'

3. [Yaḥyā] related to me, from Mālik, from Nāfiʿ, that ʿAbdallāh ibn ʿUmar would say: 'No *zakāt* is due on any money until [its owner] has had it for a year.'

4. [Yaḥyā] related to me from Mālik, that Ibn Shihāb said: 'The first one to take *zakāt* [directly] out of people's stipends [i.e. the *zakāt* that he considered due on the stipend itself][36] was Muʿāwiya ibn Abī Sufyān.'

5. Mālik said: 'The *sunna* about which there is no difference of opinion among us is that *zakāt* is due on twenty dinars of gold in the same way that it is due on two hundred dirhams [of silver].'

6. Mālik said: 'There is no *zakāt* due on twenty dinars of clearly defective weight. If the amount increases so that it comes to twenty dinars of full weight, then there is *zakāt* to pay on it, but there is no *zakāt* on less than twenty dinars [of full weight]. Nor is there any *zakāt* due on two hundred dirhams of clearly defective weight. If the amount increases so that it comes to two hundred dirhams of full weight, then there is *zakāt* to pay on it. If [the dinars or dirhams] are considered acceptable in the same way that full-weight ones are (*fa-in kānat tajūzu bi-jawāz al-wāzina*) [i.e. with, at worst, only marginal weight deficiency],[37] then I think there is *zakāt* to be paid on that amount, whether it is dinars or dirhams.'

7. Mālik said, about a man who has one hundred and sixty full-weight dirhams and the exchange rate in [his] town is eight dirhams to the dinar,

that there is no *zakāt* due on [that amount]. Rather, *zakāt* is only due on twenty actual dinars or two hundred dirhams.

8. Mālik said, about a man who has five dinars, acquired as profit (*fā᾿ida*) or in some other way, and then trades with that amount until, when a year has elapsed, the amount has reached a zakātable amount, that he should pay *zakāt* on it, even if it only reaches that amount one day before the year has elapsed or one day after the year has elapsed. There is then no *zakāt* to pay on it until a year has elapsed from the day *zakāt* was paid on it.

9. Mālik said, about a man who has ten dinars and trades with them and which, by the time a year has elapsed, come to an amount of twenty dinars, that he should pay *zakāt* on that amount straightaway and not wait for a year to elapse from the time it reaches a zakātable amount, because a year has elapsed over that amount, which is now twenty dinars in his possession (*li-anna al-ḥawl qad ḥāla ʿalayhā wa-hiya ʿindahu ʿishrūn*). After that there is no *zakāt* to pay on it until a year has elapsed from the time when *zakāt* was paid on it.

10. Mālik said: 'The agreed-upon position here, with regard to income from hiring out slaves, or renting out properties, or the payments made by *mukātab* slaves, is that no *zakāt* is due on any of that until a year has elapsed from the day when the owner [of the money] takes possession of it.'

11. Mālik said, about gold and silver that is shared between partners, that if the portion of any one of them reaches twenty dinars in gold or two hundred dirhams [in silver], he should pay *zakāt* on it. If a person's portion is less than the amount on which *zakāt* is due, he does not have to pay any *zakāt*. If their portions together come to a zakātable amount, but some of them have larger portions than others, *zakāt* should be taken from each one of them according to the size of his portion, as long as each individual's share is large enough for *zakāt* to be due on it. This is because the Prophet, may Allah bless him and grant him peace, said: 'There is no *zakāt* on less than five *ūqiyya*s of silver.' Mālik added: 'This is what I prefer most out of what I have heard about this.'

12. Mālik said: 'If a man has [an amount of] gold or silver which is divided up between a number of different people, he should add it all up together and then pay whatever *zakāt* is due on the whole amount.'

13. Mālik said: 'No-one has to pay *zakāt* on gold or silver that he has acquired (*afāda*) until a year has elapsed from the day he acquired it.'[38]

In the transmission of al-Zuhrī, these thirteen reports appear in exactly the same order and almost exactly the same form. The only differences are minimal and relate to occasional slightly different formulations of the same meaning, such as using a different form of the verb but with the same meaning (e.g. Yaḥyā: *aslama ilayhi* ('gives/hands over to him'); al-Zuhrī: *sallama ilayhi*), or the inclusion or exclusion of a definite article (Yaḥyā: *min mālin zakātan*; al-Zuhrī: *min mālin al-zakāta*), or a different conditional particle (Yaḥyā: *fa-idhā qāla*; al-Zuhrī: *fa-in qāla*), or a slightly different word order (Yaḥyā: *zakāta dhālika l-māl* ('the *zakāt* of that money'); al-Zuhrī: *zakāta mālihi dhālika* ('the *zakāt* of that money of his')). Also, in al-Zuhrī's transmission, Mālik's comment 'This is what I prefer most out of what I have heard about this' becomes shortened to 'This is what I prefer most out of what I have heard'. Otherwise, the texts are effectively word for word the same.[39]

Ibn Bukayr's transmission tells almost exactly the same story. The illustrated fragment – which goes up to the end of Report No. 8 above – contains the same sort of minor differences, such as different verbs with the same meaning (where Yaḥyā and al-Zuhrī have *dafaʿa ilayya*, Ibn Bukayr has *aslama ilayya* – although, for the phrase mentioned in the previous paragraph, Ibn Bukayr, like al-Zuhrī, has *sallama ilayhi*), or slightly different formulations of the same phrase (e.g. Ibn Bukayr: *wa-in kānat tajūzu*; Yaḥyā: *fa-in kānat tajūzu*; al-Zuhrī: *wa-in kāna yajūzu*), and so forth. Ibn Bukayr also uses the shorter phrase 'The *sunna* among us' as opposed to the longer formula 'The *sunna* about which there is no difference of opinion among us' of Yaḥyā and al-Zuhrī.[40] Otherwise, Ibn Bukayr's transmission is remarkably close to the other two (and particularly that of al-Zuhrī).

The fragment of Suwayd's transmission only includes two of these thirteen reports, namely, Nos 3 and 4 above. Both of these reports are the same as in the other three transmissions mentioned, except that in No. 4, Suwayd's transmission gives simply 'Muʿāwiya' rather than 'Muʿāwiya ibn Abī Sufyān'.[41]

Al-Shaybānī's transmission is again, as in the first chapter considered above, rather different. He includes Reports Nos 1, 2 and 3, but in a different order and under different headings. Under the heading 'When is *zakāt* due on money?' he includes the *ḥadīth* from ʿAbdallāh ibn ʿUmar, that is, No. 3 above, after which he adds the comment: 'This is what we go by, and it is the opinion of Abū Ḥanīfa, except if [a person] acquires money and adds it to an amount he already has on which *zakāt* needs to be paid. Then, when *zakāt* is due on the first amount, he pays *zakāt* on the second amount along with [the first].' He then includes Reports Nos 1 and 2, in that order, under the different heading of 'If a man is owed a debt, does he have to pay *zakāt* on it?' After the first report, he adds the comment: 'We go by this, and [this] is the opinion of Abū Ḥanīfa.' None of the nine opinions of Mālik are included in al-Shaybānī's transmission.[42]

These differences can be tabulated as in Table 2.

If we consider the whole of the Book of *Zakāt* in the transmissions available, a much clearer picture emerges of both the differences in content between them and also of the general structure of the *Muwaṭṭa'* as a whole. If for convenience's sake we take Yaḥyā's transmission as the standard, we note that there are thirty separate chapters, all with their separate titles, in the Book of *Zakāt*. Al-Zuhrī's transmission contains almost exactly the same amount of material, but two of

Table 2 Differences between the Transmissions in the Book of *Zakāt*

ZAKĀT	**Yaḥyā**	**al-Zuhrī**	**Ibn Bukayr**	**Suwayd**	**al-Shaybānī**
Z 1.1 (P)	•	•	•	•	×
Z 1.2 (P)	•	•	•	•	•
Z 1.3 (S)	•	•	•	-	×
Z 1. 3a (S)	×	×	•	-	×
Z 1.4 (M)	•	•	•	-	× + AH
Z 2.1 (C)	•	•	•	-	•
Z 2.2 (C)	•	•	•	-	• + AH
Z 2.3 (C)	•	•	•	•	• + AH
Z 2.4 (C)	•	•	•	•	×
Z 2.5 (M)	•	•	•	-	×
Z 2.6 (M)	•	•	•	-	×
Z 2.7 (M)	•	•	•	-	×
Z 2.8 (M)	•	•	•	-	×
Z 2.9 (M)	•	•	-	-	×
Z 2.10 (M)	•	•	-	-	×
Z 2.11 (M)	•	•	-	-	×
Z 2.12 (M)	•	•	-	-	×
Z 2.13 (M)	•	•	-	-	×

KEY:
P = Prophetic *ḥadīth*; C = Companion *ḥadīth*; M = opinion of Mālik; AH = opinion of Abū Ḥanīfa
• = present; × = not present; – = not covered by fragment

the headings in Yaḥyā's transmission are not present in al-Zuhrī's, thus leaving only twenty-eight chapters in al-Zuhrī's transmission rather than thirty as in Yaḥyā's. There is a further difference: Yaḥyā's transmission contains one chapter heading (his twenty-sixth: 'Buying *zakāt* and taking it back') which does not appear in al-Zuhrī's Book of *Zakāt*. It consists of two Prophetic reports, followed by an opinion of Mālik.[43] The opinion of Mālik appears, although in a modified form, elsewhere in al-Zuhrī's Book of *Zakāt* (towards the end of his tenth chapter);[44] and while the two Prophetic *ḥadīth*s do not appear in the Book of *Zakāt* in al-Zuhrī's transmission, they do appear in al-Zuhrī's Book of Jihad.[45] Al-Zuhrī's transmission also contains one chapter heading, 'Taking [livestock from the people of] *jizya* as part of their *jizya* (poll-tax)', which does not appear in Yaḥyā's transmission. In al-Zuhrī's transmission this chapter contains three reports: two Companion reports (from ʿUmar) and one opinion of Mālik.[46] The second report from ʿUmar and the opinion of Mālik occur in Yaḥyā's twenty-fourth chapter, 'The *jizya* of the People of the Book and the Magians', but the first report from ʿUmar does not occur in Yaḥyā's transmission.[47] (It does, however, occur in al-Shaybānī's transmission.)[48]

If we consider the other transmissions for which extensive fragments are available, similar observations can be made. The fragment of al-Qaʿnabī's transmission contains two portions with material from the Book of *Zakāt*. The first follows Yaḥyā's transmission report by report, from the end of the chapter on 'What has come down about the *zakāt* of cattle' (Yaḥyā's twelfth chapter) to the end of the following chapter ('The *zakāt* of associates'). The second portion, which covers two chapters in both transmissions (Yaḥyā's twenty-eighth and twenty-ninth chapters), also follows Yaḥyā's transmission report by report, except that, towards the end of the first of these two chapters, al-Qaʿnabī includes an extra report from ʿUrwa ibn al-Zubayr.[49]

Suwayd's transmission, as we mentioned above, contains only fourteen reports in his chapter on 'What has come down about *zakāt*',[50] corresponding to material in eight of Yaḥyā's chapters. As there is very little material reflecting Mālik's own opinions, one might be tempted to think that, as with al-Shaybānī, this material has been edited out. However, the thirteenth of Suwyad's reports is an opinion of Mālik, and many other chapters in his transmission contain opinions of Mālik. It therefore seems that the limited extent of the material in Suwayd's Book of *Zakāt* must be due to other causes.

Al-Shaybānī's transmission shows the most differences. The twenty-three reports that he includes in his 'Chapters on *Zakāt*' are all the same as in other transmissions but are not presented in the same order (although there is a certain amount of overlap). Furthermore, as we have noted above, he also includes opinions of Abū Ḥanīfa (at least one, and sometimes more than one, in all but one of the fourteen 'Chapters on *Zakāt*').[51]

A second example will further illustrate the nature of the differences between these transmissions.

Example 2: From the Book of Fasting

In the transmission of Yaḥyā ibn Yaḥyā al-Laythi, the first three chapters of the Book of Fasting appear as follows:

> (i) *What has come down about sighting the new moon to start and end the fast in Ramadan*
>
> 1. Yaḥyā related to me from Mālik, from Nāfi', from 'Abdallāh ibn 'Umar, that the Messenger of Allah, may Allah bless him and grant him peace, mentioned Ramadan and said: 'Don't begin the fast until you see the new moon, and don't break the fast until you see the new moon. If it is cloudy, work out [when it should be].'
>
> 2. [Yaḥyā] related to me, from Mālik, from 'Abdallāh ibn Dīnār, from 'Abdallāh ibn 'Umar, that the Messenger of Allah, may Allah bless him and grant him peace, said: 'A month has [at least] twenty-nine days in it, so don't begin the fast until you see the new moon and don't break the fast until you see it. If it is cloudy, work out [when it should be].'
>
> 3. [Yaḥyā] related to me, from Mālik, from Thawr ibn Zayd al-Dīlī, from 'Abdallāh ibn 'Abbās, that the Messenger of Allah, may Allah bless him and grant him peace, mentioned Ramadan and said: 'Don't begin the fast until you see the new moon, and don't break the fast until you see the new moon. If it is cloudy, complete a full thirty days.'
>
> 4. [Yaḥyā] related to me, from Mālik, that he had heard that the new moon was once sighted in the time of 'Uthmān in the late afternoon and 'Uthmān did not break the fast until it was evening and the sun had set.
>
> 5. Yaḥyā said: I heard Mālik say, about someone who saw the new moon of Ramadan by himself, that he should fast, and that it was not correct for

him to break the fast when he knew that that day was part of Ramadan. He added: 'Whoever sees the new moon of Shawwāl by himself should not break the fast, because the danger with people is that someone among them who is not trustworthy will break the fast, and then others, when they hear about this, will say 'We have seen the new moon.' Whoever sees the new moon of Shawwāl during the day [i.e. before sunset] should not break the fast but should complete that day's fasting, because that is the new moon of the coming night.'

6. Yaḥyā said: I heard Mālik say: 'If people are fasting on the Day of Fiṭr, thinking that it is Ramadan, and then hear from a reliable source that the new moon of Ramadan was seen a day before they [themselves] started fasting and that that day is now Day 31, they should break their fast, on that day, at whatever time the news reaches them. However, they should not do the ʿĪd prayer if the news comes to them after mid-day.'

(ii) *Making the intention to fast before dawn*

1. Yaḥyā related to me, from Mālik, from Nafiʿ, that ʿAbdallāh ibn ʿUmar would say: 'Only someone who has made the intention to fast before dawn is actually fasting.' [Yaḥyā, al-Zuhrī, al-Shaybānī: *lā yasūmu … illā*;[52] Ibn Bukayr, Suwayd: *lā yasūmanna … illā*].[53]

2. [Yaḥyā] related to me, from Mālik, from Ibn Shihāb, the same as that from ʿĀʾisha and Ḥafṣa, the wives of the Prophet, may Allah bless him and grant him peace.

(iii) *What has come down about being quick to break the fast*

1. Yaḥyā related to me, from Mālik, from Abū Hāzim ibn Dīnār, from Sahl ibn Saʿd al-Sāʿidī, that the Messenger of Allah, may Allah bless him and grant him peace, said: 'People will remain in good as long as they are quick to break the fast.'

2. [Yaḥyā] related to me, from Mālik, from ʿAbd al-Raḥmān ibn Ḥarmala al-Aslamī, from Saʿīd ibn al-Musayyab, that the Messenger of Allah, may Allah bless him and grant him peace, said: 'People will remain in good as long as they are quick to break the fast.'

3. [Yaḥyā] related to me, from Mālik, from Ibn Shihāb, from Ḥumayd ibn ʿAbd al-Raḥmān, that ʿUmar ibn al-Khaṭṭāb and ʿUthmān ibn ʿAffān would both pray maghrib when they saw the night darkening, before breaking their fast, and would then break their fast after doing the prayer. That was in Ramadan.[54]

The first chapter thus contains six reports: three Prophetic *ḥadīth*s of very similar import, one report from ʿUthmān ibn ʿAffān and two opinions of Mālik; the second contains two Companion reports, with the same content, from three different authorities; and the third contains two Prophetic *ḥadīth*s, only differing in their *isnād*, and a further report about the practice of ʿUmar and ʿUthmān.

In the transmission of al-Zuhrī, all these reports occur, and in the same order, except that he includes a further short chapter, containing three reports, between the first two chapters, as follows:

What has come down about the pre-dawn meal *(suhūr)*

1. Abū Muṣʿab related to us, saying: Mālik related to us, from Ibn Shihāb, from Sālim ibn ʿAbdallāh ibn ʿUmar, that the Messenger of Allah, may Allah bless him and grant him peace, said: 'Bilāl calls [the *adhān*] while it is still night, so eat and drink until Ibn Umm Maktūm calls [the *adhān*].' [Ibn Shihāb] said: 'Ibn Umm Maktūm was a blind man, who wouldn't call [the *adhān*] until someone had said to him "Morning has come. Morning has come." '

2. Abū Muṣʿab related to us, saying: Mālik related to us, from ʿAbdallāh ibn Dīnār, from ʿAbdallāh ibn ʿUmar, that the Messenger of Allah, may Allah bless him and grant him peace, said: 'Bilāl calls [the *adhān*] while it is still night, so eat and drink until Ibn Umm Maktūm calls [the *adhān*].'

3. Abū Muṣʿab related to us, saying: Mālik related to us that he heard ʿAbd al-Karīm ibn Abī l-Mukhāriq say: 'Part of the practice of the prophets (*min ʿamal al-nubuwwa*) is being quick to break the fast and delaying the pre-dawn meal.'[55]

These three reports all occur in the transmission of Yaḥyā ibn Yaḥyā al-Laythi, but in other places. The first two occur in the Book of the Prayer, in the chapter entitled 'The time of *suhūr* in relation to the call to prayer',[56] and the third occurs, in an extended form, in the Book of Shortening the Prayer, in the chapter entitled 'Placing one hand over the other in the prayer'.[57] (All three are repeated in the equivalent places in al-Zuhrī's transmission.)[58]

In the transmission of Ibn Bukayr, all these four chapters occur in the same order as they appear in al-Zuhrī's transmission and with the same content – the only significant difference being a different *isnād* for the first *ḥadīth* in the chapter on 'Being quick to break the fast' which, instead of being from Abū Ḥāzim ibn Dīnār, from Sahl (as in the transmissions of Yaḥyā and al-Zuhrī; also those of al-Qa'nabī, Suwayd, and al-Shaybānī), is from Ibn Shihāb, from Sālim ibn 'Abdallāh ibn 'Umar.[59] The fragment of al-Qa'nabī's transmission also has the same reports, and in the same order, but the fragment only contains the material from the fourth report in the first chapter (about 'Uthmān) through to the second report in the third chapter (from 'Abd al-Raḥmān ibn Ḥarmala).[60] Suwayd's transmission is close to these last three: it contains all the *ḥadīths* in these four chapters, and in the same order, except that he omits – or seems to have omitted – the Companion *ḥadīth* from 'Uthmān and the opinions of Mālik in the first chapter.[61] Al-Shaybānī's transmission is more truncated: he avoids repetitions of content in the Prophetic material but maintains the Companion material; he also omits the opinions of Mālik but includes instead opinions of Abū Ḥanīfa.[62] (See Table 3.)

As in the example of *zakāt* above, there are a few minor differences on a purely formal level between the transmissions which do not affect the meaning. Names may be shortened. For example, 'Abdallāh ibn 'Umar is given

Table 3 Differences between the Transmissions in the Book of Fasting

FASTING	Yaḥyā	al-Zuhrī	Ibn Bukayr	al-Qa'nabī	Suwayd	al-Shaybānī
F 1.1 (P)	•	•	•	-	•	• + AH
F 1.2 (P)	•	•	•	-	•	(•)
F 1.3 (P)	•	•	•	-	•	×
F 1.4 (C)	•	•	•	•	×	×
F 1.5 (M)	•	•	•	•	×	×
F 1.6 (M)	•	•	•	•	×	×
F 2.1 (P)	›	•	•	•	•	• + AH
F 2.2 (P)	›	•	•	•	•	×
F 2.3 (P)	›	•	•	•	•	×
F 3.1 (P)	•	•	•	•	•	• + AH
F 3.2 (P)	•	•	•	•	•	×
F 3.3 (P)	•	•	•	-	•	• + (AH)
F 4.1 (C)	•	•	•	-	•	• + AH
F 4.2 (C)	•	•	-	-	×	×

KEY:
P = Prophetic *ḥadīth*; C = Companion *ḥadīth*; M = opinion of Mālik; AH = opinion of Abū Ḥanīfa
• = present; › = elsewhere; × = not present; – not covered by fragment

sometimes as simply Ibn ʿUmar (e.g. Suwayd: first two *ḥadīth*s), Ḥumayd ibn ʿAbd al-Raḥmān ibn ʿAwf (Ibn Bukayr) is given as simply Ḥumayd ibn ʿAbd al-Raḥmān (the others), and ʿAbd al-Karīm ibn Abī l-Mukhāriq al-Baṣrī (Yaḥyā) is given simply as ʿAbd al-Karīm ibn Abī l-Mukhāriq in the transmissions of al-Zuhrī, Ibn Bukayr, al-Qaʿnabī and Suwayd. There are also one or two examples of additional text in some transmissions, for example, 'That was in Ramadan' (Yaḥyā, al-Zuhrī, Ibn Bukayr, al-Qaʿnabī, but not in the transmission of Suwayd) and, more significantly perhaps, in the *ḥadīth* from ʿAbd al-Raḥmān ibn Ḥarmala (*Ḥadīth* 3.2 above), where the additional phrase 'they should not delay it like the people of the East do' occurs in the transmissions of al-Zuhrī, Ibn Bukayr, al-Qaʿnabī and Suwayd, but not in that of Yaḥyā.[63] Sometimes, as we saw in the example about *zakāt*, a slightly different grammatical form is used, for example, *lā yasūmu* (approx. 'he is not fasting') (Yaḥyā, al-Zuhrī, al-Shaybānī) as opposed to *lā yasūmanna* (approx. 'he should not fast') (Ibn Bukayr, Suwayd).

It is thus apparent that, for this portion of the text at least, the transmissions of al-Zuhrī, Ibn Bukayr and al-Qaʿnabī are remarkably similar, and that of Yaḥyā ibn Yaḥyā only marginally different. (Suwayd's transmission here is also close to the first three.) Any differences that there are are only minor and have no bearing on the basic framework and meaning of the texts being transmitted. Even al-Shaybānī's transmission, while omitting some reports – notably the opinions of Mālik – and including others – notably the opinions of Abū Ḥanīfa – nevertheless shares a large amount of the basic material that is clearly recognizable as being part of 'the *Muwaṭṭa*ʾ'.

If we broaden our focus to cover the whole of the Book of Fasting, we find a similar situation as with the Book of *Zakāt*. In Yaḥyā's transmission, the Book of Fasting contains twenty-two chapters, although there is some related material – about fasting on the day of ʿArafa and during the days of Minā – that he includes in his Book of Ḥajj.[64] Again, al-Zuhrī's transmission contains very much the same material, but in a slightly different order: the material on fasting during the *ḥajj* is included by him in his Book of Fasting, but he mentions the material again in what he calls the Book of Rites (*Kitāb al-Manāsik*).[65]

When we look at the transmission of al-Qaʿnabī, the similarities with that of al-Zuhrī are very apparent. Al-Qaʿnabī – for the three portions from the Book of Fasting included in the published fragment of his transmission – presents the same reports and follows the same order as al-Zuhrī, the only difference being that he includes an extra report in the chapter on 'Making an oath to fast' which is not included in the transmission al-Zuhrī (but is in the transmission of Yaḥyā), and that he includes material on fasting during *ḥajj* in the Book of Fasting.[66]

The fragment of Suwayd's transmission includes a much more extensive portion of the Book of Fasting than it does of the Book of *Zakāt*. Altogether he includes seventy-one reports, which, except for two minor reversals of order, follow exactly the same order as the transmissions of al-Zuhrī and, where the relevant fragments overlap, of al-Qaʿnabī.[67]

Al-Shaybānī's transmission, as we saw above in the case of the Book of *Zakāt*, contains significantly less material and in a significantly different order.[68] Nevertheless, all the reports from Mālik that he includes in his transmission are represented in one or more of the other transmissions. The main difference, as we saw with the Book of *Zakāt*, is that he excludes any opinions of Mālik and, instead, includes opinions of Abū Ḥanīfa, with the comment 'This is what we go by'.

It thus seems that the transmissions of al-Zuhrī and al-Qaʿnabī – and Ibn Bukayr to the extent that one has had access to his transmission – are remarkably close to each other, only differing – and then only occasionally – on minor details of vocabulary, grammar and/or word order and the order of presentation. Yaḥyā's varies a little more, but is nevertheless very close to them.[69] Suwayd's transmission is also very close to these others – certainly textually speaking – although not as complete; and, while al-Shaybānī's transmission is more pruned, it is nevertheless, textually speaking, very much part of the cluster of material transmitted from Mālik under the umbrella of 'the *Muwaṭṭa*'.[70]

It will be evident that all of these differences are minor and have no bearing on the basic texts being transmitted, all of which goes to confirm, as we noted earlier, the attribution of the material to the person the transmitters say they got it from – Mālik – in the place where he was living – Medina. The varied and broad geographical distribution of these transmitters – Yaḥyā in al-Andalus

(Spain), al-Zuhrī in Medina, Ibn Bukayr in Egypt, al-Qaʿnabī in Basra, Suwayd in al-Haditha (Iraq) and al-Shaybānī in Kufa (Iraq) – not to mention also Ibn al-Qāsim in Egypt and Ibn Ziyād in Tunis – also acts as a confirmation of this claim: it would have been extremely difficult, if not impossible, for them to have got together to make up a lie – indeed, innumerable lies – about Mālik, which then everyone else not only accepted as true but were also prepared to act upon in their everyday lives because of that acceptance. The many transmissions of this corpus of texts – not to mention their indirect transmission in the standard *ḥadīth* literature (such as the well-known Six Books) – all corroborate each other and indicate a highly reliable text.

In short, in the *Muwaṭṭa'* of Mālik we have a very strong textual tradition which – excepting only the Qur'an – is unparalleled in the history of Islam, thus justifying al-Shāfiʿī's comment (see above) that the *Muwaṭṭa'* is the most accurate book on the face of the earth after the Qur'an.

The form and general content of the *Muwaṭṭa'*

But what was it that this book contained? We have seen, in the examples outlined above, that it contains four main categories of material. There are *ḥadīths* from the Prophet, there are reports from various Companions, there are reports from various Successors, and there are reports – often introduced as 'opinions' – from Mālik. Furthermore, in any one chapter they are presented in that order: that is, where there are reports from all four categories, it is the Prophetic *ḥadīths* that are put first, then Companion and Successor *ḥadīths*, and then, finally, any general statements by Mālik. We can thus assume that this material is being presented in order of precedence, with material from or about the Prophet occupying pride of place, then material from the Companions, then the Successors and then Mālik. At the same time, this represents a chronological arrangement, with the historical sequence of Prophet-Companions-Successors-Mālik being preserved, which, of course, also appears more specifically in the individual *isnāds* (chains of authority) of these reports. In other words, there is a continuity of transmission, from the Prophet, through the Companions and Successors, up to the time of Mālik.

This continuity is made even more apparent by the presence among Mālik's opinions of phrases such as 'What has been established as *sunna*', 'This is what the people of knowledge in our city have always held to' and 'This is the position that the people of knowledge have always held to here'. This indicates a continuous transmission of this material, not by text, but by *ʿamal*, or action, from the time of the Prophet up until to the time of Imam Mālik.

It is recorded that Mālik was once asked about these and similar expressions, such as 'The agreed position here', or '… in our city', 'I found the people of knowledge [doing] …', or 'I heard some of the people of knowledge [saying] …', and he said,

> Most of what is in the book is my opinion, but, on my life, it is not so much my opinion as that which I have heard from more than one of the people of knowledge and excellence and the imams worthy of being followed from whom I took my knowledge – and they were God-fearing. But, in order to simplify matters I have said it is my opinion. This [I have done] when their opinion was the same as that which they found the Companions following, and which I then found them [i.e. the Successors] following. It is thus an inheritance which has been passed down from one generation to another down to our present time. [So] when I say, 'I am of the opinion', it is really the opinion of a large group of the imams who have gone before. When I say, 'The agreed upon position with us', it is what the people of *fiqh* and knowledge have agreed upon without any difference of opinion among them. When I say, 'The position with us (*al-amr ʿindanā*)', it is what the people here have acted upon, and has become the basis for judgements, and is known by both the learned and the ignorant. Similarly, when I have said, 'in our city', or 'some of the people of knowledge', that is something that I have considered good (*istaḥsantuhu*) among the opinions (*qawl*) of the people of knowledge. Where I have heard nothing from them, I have used my own judgement (*ijtahadtu*) and considered the matter according to the way (*madhhab*) of those I have met, until I felt that I had arrived at the truth, or near to it, so that it would not be outside the way of the people of Medina and their opinions, even though I had not heard that particular [judgement] directly.
>
> I have thus said that it is my opinion after having considered the matter deeply in relation to the *sunna* and what has been endorsed by the people of knowledge who are worthy of being followed, and what the practice here

> has been from the time of the Messenger of Allah, may Allah bless him and grant him peace, and the Rightly-Guided Caliphs, along with what those who I have met in my life-time [have said]. It is thus their opinion, and I have not gone outside it for anyone else's.[71]

Such phrases – 'This is the position here with us', or 'This is the *sunna* about which there is no disagreement here with us, and which the practice of the people (*ʿamal al-nās*) is still in accord with', and others of the same ilk – also indicate that this transmission took place in Medina ('with us') and manifested itself in the actions of the people of Medina. This, then, is how the people of Medina were putting the judgements of the Sharīʿa into practice. This is the concept of the *ʿamal* of the people of Medina, which is the keystone of Mālik's *madhhab*, or way of arriving at legal judgements. It is to this that we now turn.

4

The *ʿamal* of the people of Medina

We have noted above that an understanding of the *ʿamal* of the people of Medina is critical to an understanding of Mālik and his way (*madhhab*) and, indeed, of the nature of his book the *Muwaṭṭaʾ*. We have seen that it is in the nature of the *Muwaṭṭaʾ* to include *ḥadīth*, both Prophetic and also post-Prophetic (i.e. reports from the Companions and the Successors), but that the book encompasses more than just *ḥadīth*. It is, in effect, a sourcebook of *ʿamal*, or, one could say, a textual version of the non-textual source of *ʿamal*.

ʿAmal is a simple enough word in Arabic. It refers to action, or what is done (*ʿamila, yaʿmalu*, 'to do'). In our present context, it refers to the actions, or practice, of the people of Medina, that is, how they put the injunctions of the Qur'an and the Prophet into practice. Thus the *ʿamal* of the people of Medina is a non-textual transmission of the knowledge of the *dīn* in its practical application and refers to what the people were doing by way of putting the precepts and principles of the *dīn* into practice.

That Mālik and his contemporaries knew and used the term *ʿamal* is clear from the *Muwaṭṭaʾ* itself. A digital search of Yaḥyā's transmission reveals forty-five instances of the word *ʿamal* being used in a technical sense to refer to the *ʿamal* of the people of Medina. These instances further divide into four distinct categories:

(i) There are thirty instances of where the word *ʿamal* is used in a title heading, where the word indicates the practice (*ʿamal*) or procedure that should be followed, that is, 'what is [to be] done' in a particular situation, such as 'The practice (*al-ʿamal*) regarding doing *ghusl* for the two ʿĪds and calling an *adhān* or *iqāma* for them', where it is reported that Mālik had heard 'more than one of their scholars say that there has never been any call to prayer or *iqāma* for [the prayers of] ʿĪd al-Fiṭr or ʿĪd al-Aḍḥā from the time of the Messenger of Allah, may Allah bless him and grant him peace, up until today';[1] or 'The practice regarding the *ʿaqīqa* sacrifice [i.e. the sacrifice for a new-born child]', where Mālik says,

> The way things are done here (*al-amr ʿindanā*) with regard to the *ʿaqīqa* sacrifice is that, if anyone slaughters for this purpose, he does so by slaughtering one sheep for either a male or female child. The *ʿaqīqa* sacrifice is not obligatory, but it is a recommended action (*yustaḥabb al-ʿamal bi-hā*), and is part of the way people have always done things here.[2]

In the section on *ʿaqīqa* in Ibn Ziyād's transmission, Mālik refers to the practice of sacrificing one sheep per child, whether for a boy or a girl, and uses the direct expression 'This is the practice (*al-ʿamal*) here'.[3]

(ii) There are six instances where it is denied that a particular judgement is the ongoing practice (*ʿamal*), such as Saʿd ibn Abī Waqqāṣ doing only one *rakʿa* (instead of three) for *witr*, after which Mālik comments that 'the practice with us does not accord with this';[4] or Mālik's comment, with regard to a decision of ʿUmar to double the compensation price that was owed for a camel that had been stolen and then slaughtered, 'It is not the practice here with us (*wa-laysa ʿalā hādhā l-ʿamalu ʿindnā*) to double the compensation price; rather, the established practice of the people here is that the man pays, as a fine, the value of the camel or animal on the day that he took it.'[5]

(iii) There are five instances of where a practice is stated as being the ongoing practice (*ʿamal*), such as the instance of the *ʿaqīqa* sacrifice referred to above – 'this is the practice (*ʿamal*) here'; or where Mālik says that, if date palms are shared between two people and the harvest of one of them, but not the other, reaches the minimum amount on which *zakāt* is due, only the one who harvests that minimum has to pay *zakāt*. 'This,' he says, 'is the practice (*al-ʿamal*) with regard to all associates in any crop that is harvested.'[6]

(iv) There are also four instances where the expression 'the practice of the people (*ʿamal al-nās*)' – or, in one case, 'the practice of those who have gone before (*ʿamal al-māḍīn*)' – is used, all of which indicate that a certain practice was the general practice of the people which was well known and accepted among them. Thus, for instance, Mālik notes that it is permitted for someone to buy an animal and pay for it in advance, as long as the date for payment is specified, the animal is clearly described and the price is paid upfront; this is then binding on both parties. 'This,' he says, 'continues to be part of the practice of the people (*ʿamal al-nās*) which is acceptable (*jāʾiz*) between them and which the people of knowledge in our city continue to hold to.'[7] Similarly, Mālik notes that selling bundles according to a list of their contents is different from selling a head-and-shoulder cloth (*sāj*/*ṭaylasān*) in its bag, or a garment which is folded up, or suchlike. The difference, he says, is

> the way things are done (*al-amr al-maʿmūl bihi*) and the knowledge of this that people have in their hearts, and the practice of those who have gone before (*ʿamal al-māḍīn*), and that this continues to be a type of transaction that people consider acceptable and see no harm in. [This is] because selling bundles according to a list of their contents, without displaying everything, is not done with any intention of [benefitting from] uncertainty (*gharar*).[8]

It is thus clear that, for Mālik's time at least, the principle and concept of *ʿamal* was very much used and acknowledged and not a later theoretical construct.[9]

There has been a lot of dispute about this source from the earliest times. Because by concept it is a non-textual source, it immediately poses problems for those with a textual frame of reference – and that means most scholars throughout most of Islamic history. For, although the Prophet was 'unlettered' (*ummī*), that is, did not read or write, his teachings became progressively recorded in written form: first in the form of the Qur'an, as the message delivered by him in his capacity as the Messenger of Allah, and then, later, in the form of *ḥadīth*, as a record of his sayings and actions in his capacity as the first exemplar of this Qur'anic message. Indeed, 'knowledge' in the early period of Islamic history effectively meant 'knowledge of *ḥadīth*'. But, as we have also seen, for Mālik there was something else that was more reliable, and in this sense higher, than *ḥadīth*, namely, the practice of the *dīn* in his native city of Medina. The very name Medina means, quite literally – according to the view that it is the noun of place of the root *dāna*, *yadīnu* – the place of the *dīn*, that is, the place where it was put into practice. In a letter to al-Layth ibn Saʿd (d. 175/791), Mālik himself said about Medina and its people,

> All people are subordinate to the people of Medina. To it the Emigration was made, in it the Qur'an was revealed and the lawful (*ḥalāl*) made lawful and the forbidden (*ḥarām*) made forbidden. The Messenger of Allah was living

> among them and they were present during the very act of revelation. He would tell them to do things and they would obey him. He would institute *sunna*s for them and they would follow him, until Allah took him to Himself and chose for him what is in His presence, may the blessings and mercy of Allah be upon him.
>
> Then there rose up after him those who were put in authority after him and who, of his community, were the ones who followed him most closely. When matters arose about which they had knowledge, they put that knowledge into practice. If they did not have [the requisite] knowledge, they would ask [others] and would go by what they considered the most valid option according to their own personal reasoning (*ijtihād*) and their recent experience [of when the Prophet was alive]. If someone disagreed with them, or said something that was more valid and more worthy of being followed, they would leave aside their own opinion and act according to the other, stronger opinion. After them the Successors trod the same path and followed the same *sunna*s.
>
> So, if there is something clearly acted upon in Medina, I am not of the opinion that anyone may go against it, because of the inheritance that [the Medinans] have which it is not permissible for any others to ascribe to, or claim for, themselves. Even if the people of other cities were to say, 'This is the practice (*ʿamal*) in our city', or 'This is what those before us used to do [here]', they would not have the same authority for that, nor would it be permissible for them in the way that it is for [the people of Medina].[10]

So, for Mālik, what he and the people of his city had inherited was the practice of Islam, and it had the authority of all those who had practised it, and kept it in practice, from the time of the Prophet, though the time of the Companions and the Successors, down to his own day. And he was concerned to pass that on, as it was, and not to go beyond them. But, by his time, other centres had grown up, or were beginning to grow up, foremost among which was that of the people of Kufa, represented particularly by Imam Abū Ḥanīfa and his two main students, Abū Yūsuf and al-Shaybānī (al-Shaybānī being, as we have seen, one of Mālik's own students and a transmitter of a version of the *Muwaṭṭaʾ*). In a short space of time these two positions, those of Medina and Kufa, would be rivalled by a third school, that of Imam al-Shāfiʿī – another student of Mālik – in Egypt.

These three schools would later become the three main *madhhab*s of the Muslim world, namely, the Mālikīs, the Ḥanafīs and the Shāfiʿīs, which, alongside a fourth *madhhab*, the Ḥanbalīs (referring to Aḥmad ibn Ḥanbal) would become the Four Madhhabs of classical Islam.

In the classical picture, all four *madhhab*s are based on certain shared sources, namely, the Qur'an, the *sunna*, consensus and analogy, and this is what creates their overall similarity. But there are other, disputed sources in addition to the agreed ones. If we take the Mālikī *madhhab* as an example, we find a number of other sources which that *madhhab* espouses, but which are generally considered disputed (i.e. disputed by some, but not necessarily all, of the other *madhhabs*). Thus, in his *Ḥāshiya* ('marginal gloss') on Mayyāra's commentary on the famous didactic poem *al-Murshid al-Muʿīn*, the Mālikī scholar Ibn Ḥamdūn (d. Fez, *c.* 1273/1856), summarizing, says,

> Mālik bases his *madhhab* on seventeen sources (*adilla*), namely:
>
> 1. an unambiguous text (*naṣṣ*) of the Qur'an;
>
> 2. its overt meaning (*ẓāhir*), by which I mean the general application (*ʿumūm*) [of a judgement];
>
> 3. its *dalīl* ('indication'), by which I mean *mafhūm al-mukhālafa* (lit. 'what is understood by contrast', i.e. *argumentum e contrario*, or counter-implication);
>
> 4. its *mafhūm* ('implication'), by which I mean *al-mafhūm bi-l-awlā* (lit. 'what is understood as being more appropriate', i.e. *a fortiori* deduction);
>
> 5. its *shabah* ('similarity'), by which I mean when the reason for a judgement is given, as when Allah says, '[except for carrion, flowing blood, or pork] because that is filth; or some deviance (*fisq*) [consecrated to other than Allah]' [Q. 6:145];
>
> 6–10. the same five with regard to the *sunna*;
>
> 11. consensus (*ijmāʿ*);
>
> 12. analogy (*qiyās*);
>
> 13. the *ʿamal* ('practice') of the people of Medina;
>
> 14. the opinion (*qawl*) of a Companion;
>
> 15. *istiḥsān* ('considerations of equity');
>
> 16. *sadd al-dharāʾiʿ* (lit. 'blocking the means [to what is *ḥarām*]'); and

17. *istiṣḥāb* (i.e. assuming the continuation of a situation, and thus of the relevant judgement).

18. As for *murāʿāt al-khilāf* ('taking the differences [between *madhhabs*] into account'), this is sometimes followed and sometimes not.[11]

This list provides a convenient overview, but it also poses problems. First, it is quite clearly a systematisation: we are presented with eighteen different categories, all of which are potentially the source for a judgement, but there is clearly overlap between them, such that, for example, the judgements about the prohibition of taking usury, or the obligation to fast Ramadan, may be found in both the Qur'an and the *sunna*, quite apart from the subdivision of Qur'an and *sunna* into the first ten categories given above. Second, it is also very much a text-based, or text-influenced, systematization. Thus, for example, the first ten categories refer to linguistic techniques of approaching the Qur'an and the *sunna, as texts.* By contrast, the *ʿamal* of the people of Medina (No. 13) is quintessentially a non-textual source, although that, too, becomes recorded historically in textual form. Third, this list creates a potentially false sense of priorities. Qur'an and *sunna* (Nos 1–10) are rightly given pride of place – we recall the *ḥadīth* that Mālik highlights in the *Muwaṭṭaʾ*: 'I have left among you two things, and if you hold to them both you will never go astray: the Book of Allah and the Sunna of His Prophet'[12] – after which come consensus and analogy (Nos 11 and 12), the other two of the accepted 'four sources'. Thus the *ʿamal* of the people of Medina, at No. 13, is effectively relegated to a subsidiary position after the four main sources, which accords with the view that it is a disputed source that is not accepted by the other *madhhab*s.

There are further issues with this 'four-sources-plus' picture. First, it was only with the work of Imam al-Shāfiʿī (d. 204/820) that the 'four-source' theory really began to take shape (he is credited with being the first to propound it – albeit in a pre-systematized form – in his renowned *Risāla*),[13] so one is entitled to ask, what was the picture that was envisaged before the time of Imam al-Shāfiʿī, that is, at the time of Imam Mālik, and before him? (We should remember that in the wording of the Qur'an the *dīn* was complete at the time of the Farewell Hajj: 'Today I have perfected your *dīn* for you, and completed My blessing on you, and am pleased with Islam as a *dīn* for you (*al-yawma akmaltu lakum dīnakum wa-atmamtu ʿalaykum niʿmatī wa-raḍītu lakumu l-islāma dīnan*)' [Q. 5:3].) Second, the *ʿamal* of the people of Medina has to be seen as more than just one source out of many (e.g. one out of 17, or possibly 18, as with Ibn Ḥamdūn above). Rather, we can see it as an all-encompassing source which effectively gives us a practical application and understanding of 'Qur'an and *sunna*'.

We also note in passing that there are some sources that, although commonly associated with Mālik and his *madhhab*, do not appear in Ibn Ḥamdūn's list, for example, *ʿurf* ('custom') and *al-maṣāliḥ al-mursala* (lit. 'untrammelled benefits' i.e. considerations of the public good when there is no clear text either for or against a particular matter).

We have seen above that Medina is seen, and remembered by its scholars, as the place where the *ḥalāl* and the *ḥarām* were revealed and where the various *sunna*s of the Prophet were first put into practice. This living picture was then inherited and passed down, by each successive generation, to the time of Mālik, whose *Muwaṭṭaʾ* can be considered as a distillation of this *dīn*-in-action that Mālik witnessed at first hand in his native city and wished to preserve and pass on to others. Mālik himself said of his book,

> In it are *ḥadīth*s of the Messenger of Allah, may Allah bless him and grant him peace, and opinions (*qawl*) of the Companions and the Successors, and opinions (*raʾy*) which are the consensus (*ijmāʿ*) of the people of Medina and whose [opinions] I have not gone beyond (*lam akhruj ʿanhum*).[14]

From the later, post-Shāfiʿī perspective, we are used to *ḥadīth* being just the *ḥadīth* of the Prophet. Thus, when we look at any of the major *ḥadīth* collections, such as the *Ṣaḥīḥ* of al-Bukhārī, for instance, we find that the overwhelming majority of the material is Prophetic, that is, it goes back specifically and overtly to the Prophet. In the *Muwaṭṭaʾ*, however, and other early collections of *ḥadīth*, this is not the case. There, by contrast, we find that at least half of the material comes from sources other than the Prophet, that is, from the Companions and the Successors. This implies that a change had taken place between the time of the compilation of the *Muwaṭṭaʾ* and other early collections of *ḥadīth*, in the second half of the second century AH, and the time of the compilation of the Six Books, beginning in the first half of the third century AH. This change is that the later compilers are no longer interested in anything other than reports with a formal – and authentic – *isnād* back to the Prophet, that is, in texts, and ones with specifically Prophetic authority. Anything else is considered insufficient, indeed 'weak'. But this was not the position of Mālik and his contemporaries for whom other reports and other information also had authority.

What was this authority? If we go back to Mālik's comment above, we notice that he says 'whose [opinions] I have not gone beyond (*lam akhruj ʿanhum*)'. By this he is indicating a different sort of transmission of knowledge, and a different sort of understanding, and transmission, of the *sunna* – one which is encompassed by the *ʿamal* of the people of Medina.

The *ʿamal* of the people of Medina

What is the *ʿamal* of the people of Medina? ʿIyāḍ says, in his *Madārik*,

> You should know, may Allah ennoble you, that all the leaders of the *madhhab*s, whether legal scholars or theologians, or people of *ḥadīth* or people of intellectual reasoning, are as one group against us regarding this matter, attributing error to us – as they claim – and using as an argument whatever occurs to them, to the extent that some of them have gone beyond the limits of prejudice and defamation and cast aspersions on Medina and listed its faults, when this is not a matter about which there is any dispute. Among them are those who have failed to understand the matter or to find out the true position of our *madhhab* with regard to it, and so have spoken about it on a basis of guesswork and conjecture; among them also are those who have taken their words from others who have not understood what our true position is; and among them are those who have altered things and have attributed to us what we would never say about the matter, as have al-Ṣayrafī, al-Maḥāmilī and al-Ghazālī, who have transmitted on our authority what we would never say, and have used as an argument against us the same arguments that are used against those who cast aspersions on consensus (*ijmāʿ*).[15]

So *ʿamal* is not to be confused with the 'standard' meaning of consensus, since the consensus of Medina is a different concept altogether. Rather, the consensus of Medina is based on the *sunna* of the Prophet, but on a non-textual, *ʿamal*-based transmission of it.

This is also why the *ʿamal* of the first generations in Medina is understood to be stronger than *ḥadīth*, that is, a better indication of *sunna*, even if those *ḥadīth* are completely authentic and backed up by the most impeccable *isnād*s. In a chapter entitled 'What has been related from the first community and the men of knowledge regarding the obligation to go back to the practice (*ʿamal*) of the People of Medina, and its being a conclusive proof in their opinion, even if it is contrary to *ḥadīth*', ʿIyāḍ spells out the argument for the superiority of *ʿamal* over *ḥadīth* as a more accurate transmission of the *sunna* of the Prophet. He says,

> It is related that ʿUmar ibn al-Khaṭṭāb, may Allah be pleased with him, once said on the *minbar*: 'By Allah, I will make things difficult for any man who relates a *ḥadīth* which is contrary to *ʿamal*.'
>
> Ibn al-Qāsim and Ibn Wahb said: 'I saw that with Mālik *ʿamal* was stronger than *ḥadīth*.'
>
> Mālik said: 'There were people among the men of knowledge of the Successors who would narrate certain *ḥadīth*s, and hear other *ḥadīth*s from others, and would say, "We are not ignorant of this, but the *ʿamal* that has come down to us is different." '
>
> Mālik said: 'I once saw Muḥammad ibn Abī Bakr ibn ʿAmr ibn Ḥazm, who was a judge, being reproached by his brother, ʿAbdallāh, who was an honest man with an extensive knowledge of *ḥadīth*, for giving a judgement on a case when there was a *ḥadīth* giving a different judgement. ʿAbdallāh said, "Hasn't such-and-such a *ḥadīth* come down about this?" Muḥammad replied, "It has." ʿAbdallāh said, "Then why don't you give your judgement in accordance with it?" Muḥammad replied, "But what is the position of the people with regard to it?" – i.e. [what is] the agreed *ʿamal* in Medina? – by which he meant that the *ʿamal* of Medina was stronger than *ḥadīth*.'

We recall (see Chapter 2) that ʿAbdallāh ibn Abī Bakr ibn ʿAmr ibn Ḥazm was one of Mālik's main teachers of *ḥadīth*. His brother Muḥammad, however, was a judge and thus involved in the daily application of the Sharīʿa, and knowledge of what was applied in practice was higher than what was only theoretical. (Muḥammad was also one of Mālik's sources, as we have seen, for some reports in the *Muwaṭṭaʾ*.) ʿIyāḍ continues,

Ibn al-Muʿadhdhal said: 'I once heard someone ask Ibn al-Mājishūn, "Why do you transmit a *ḥadīth* and then not act upon it?" He replied, "So that it be known that it is with full knowledge of it that we do not act upon it." '

Ibn Mahdī said: 'The established *sunna* of the people of Medina is better than *ḥadīth*.' He also said: 'Often I will have numerous *ḥadīth*s on a subject, but will find the people of the mosque (*ahl al-ʿarṣa*, lit. 'the people of the courtyard') following something contrary to them, at which point those *ḥadīth*s become weak in my opinion' – or words to that effect.

Rabīʿa said: 'One thousand from one thousand is preferred by me to one from one. One from one would tear the *sunna* right out of your hands.'[16]

'One thousand from one thousand' is the methodology of Medina; 'one from one' is effectively the methodology of everywhere else.

We noted above that all the Muslims accepted the primacy of 'Qur'an and *sunna*', but how was this 'Qur'an and *sunna*' to be understood? In later times, once both Qur'an and *sunna* have been thoroughly textualized, we have *tafsīr*s ('commentaries') of Qur'an and *sharḥ*s ('commentaries') of the *ḥadīth* texts, but before any *tafsīr* or *sharḥ* there was the original practice of the *dīn* – the *ʿamal* of the people of Medina – and this *ʿamal* acts as a *tafsīr* of Qur'an and a *sharḥ* of *ḥadīth*, but a living, non-textualized one that was passed on from generation to generation first and foremost by action rather than texts.

Some examples of *tafsīr* and *sharḥ* by *ʿamal*

Some examples from the *Muwaṭṭaʾ* will show how Mālik presents what is effectively *tafsīr* of Qur'an by *ʿamal*, and *sharḥ* of *sunna* by *ʿamal*.

Example 1: The oath of abstinence from marital intercourse

There is a verse in the Qur'an about *īlāʾ* (an oath of abstinence from marital intercourse) which says, 'Those who make an oath of abstinence from their wives may wait for four months: if they return (*fa-in fāʾū*) [to their wives], Allah is Forgiving and Merciful; if they decide to divorce (*wa-in ʿazamū l-ṭalāq*), Allah is All-Hearing and All-Knowing' (Q. 2:266–7).

A problem arose here with the meaning of the phrase 'if they return (*fa-in fāʾū*)': did it mean if they resume their marriage *before* the allotted period is up, or when it had finished? The answer to this question then affected the understanding of 'if they decide to divorce (*wa-in ʿazamū l-ṭalāq*)', since this also could be taken to mean if they decide on divorce either within the allotted period or when this period was up.

In his chapter on *īlāʾ* in the *Muwaṭṭaʾ*,[17] Mālik gives what had become the dominant *ʿamal* in Medina, although not all Medinan scholars had been of the same opinion. He begins the chapter by citing a report from ʿAlī to the effect that, if a man makes such an oath and the four-month period passes without him 'returning', that is, resuming marital relations with his wife, he should be formally asked whether he wishes to resume marital relations or to divorce. He then adds the characteristic phrase, 'This is the position with us (*wa-dhalika l-amr ʿindanā*)', that is, this is the judgement acted upon and the *ʿamal* of the people of Medina regarding this point. He then says that this was also the view of Ibn ʿUmar. However, he then notes that this was not the only position held in Medina: two of the well-known Seven Jurists of Medina – Saʿīd ibn al-Musayyab and Abū Bakr ibn ʿAbd al-Raḥmān – held that the 'return' had to be *within* the four-month period and that the completion of the four months constituted an automatic divorce. This, says Mālik, was also the position of Ibn Shihāb (as we have seen, one of Mālik's main teachers), as it was also the opinion that Marwān (as governor of Medina under Muʿāwiya) had gone by in adjudicating such cases. Nevertheless, despite this dissenting view – which was also the standard position of the Iraqi jurists of the early period and became the standard position of the Ḥanafī *madhhab* – the *ʿamal* of the people of Medina settled on the view of ʿAlī and Ibn ʿUmar as mentioned above. More to the point, Mālik's justification of this view in the *Muwaṭṭaʾ* is that it is 'the position with us', that is, the *ʿamal* of the people of Medina. It is then, effectively, an instance of *tafsīr* by *ʿamal*.

Example 2: Being prevented from doing *ḥajj* or *ʿumra*

Another particularly obvious example of *tafsīr* by *ʿamal* by is illustrated by the two chapters in the *Muwaṭṭaʾ* on *iḥṣār* (i.e. being prevented from doing *ḥajj* or *ʿumra*) – '*Iḥṣār* by an enemy' and '*Iḥṣār* by something ther than an enemy'.[18] The relevant Qur'anic verse does not distinguish between the two situations, saying only, 'If you are prevented, then [you should sacrifice] whatever sacrificial animal (*hady*) is easy; and do not shave your heads until the sacrificial animal has reached its place of sacrifice' (Q. 2:196). This, indeed, was the position of the Iraqi jurists, as preserved in the Ḥanafī *madhhab*. The Medinans, however, maintained the distinction recorded by Mālik in the *Muwaṭṭaʾ*: in 'ordinary' situations of *iḥṣār*, such as illness, or mistaking the beginning of the month and thus the date of the *ḥajj*, one had to follow the Qur'anic prescription of sacrificing a *hady* and shaving one's head, and so forth, *after* having reached Mecca, as laid down in Q. 2:196. If, however, one was prevented by an enemy, then the position followed by the Medinans was that of Ibn ʿUmar: 'We will do what we did with the Messenger of Allah, may Allah bless him and grant him peace …', which was simply to come out of *iḥrām* wherever one was, without having to 'reach the Kaʿba', and without having to make up the *ḥajj* or *ʿumra* at a future date or do anything else by way of reparation. This, then, is a clear instance of *tafsīr* taking the specific form of *takhṣīṣ al-qurʾān bi-l-ʿamal*, that is, making an exception to an otherwise general rule through recourse to the *ʿamal* of the people of Medina.

Example 3: How to hold one's hands when doing the prayer

A third instance illustrates how *ʿamal* could be used as a *sharḥ* of *ḥadīth*. In the *Muwaṭṭaʾ*, Mālik records two *ḥadīth*s which ostensibly indicate the judgement of *qabḍ*, that is, clasping the left hand at the wrist with the right, while doing the prayer. These two *ḥadīth*s are recorded in the chapter entitled 'Putting one hand over the other when doing the prayer', as follows:

> Yaḥyā told me, from Mālik, that ʿAbd al-Karīm ibn Abī l-Mukhāriq al-Baṣrī said: 'Among the words of prophecy are: If you do not feel ashamed, do as you wish; putting the hands one over the other when doing the prayer, that is, putting the right over the left; and hurrying to break the fast, and delaying the pre-dawn meal.'
>
> He also told me, from Mālik, from Abū Ḥāzim ibn Dīnār, that Sahl ibn Saʿd said: 'People used to be told that a man should put his right hand over his left

> arm when doing the prayer.' Abū Ḥāzim added, 'As far as I know, he traces that back [i.e. to the Prophet].'[19]

The standard position in the *madhhab*, though, as summarized for instance in Khalīl's (d. *c.* 776/1374) *Mukhtaṣar*, is that *sadl* (i.e. letting one's arms hang by one's sides) is the preferred way of doing the prayer.

As we can see, what is recorded in the *Muwaṭṭa*ʾ gives us no indication as to why *sadl* should be the preferred judgement. The *Mudawwana*, however (of which Khalīl's *Mukhtaṣar* is a summary), does. In it, Mālik is recorded (by Ibn al-Qāsim) as saying, 'I do not know about this [practice] with regard to obligatory prayers (*lā aʿrifu dhālika fī l-farīḍa*), but there is no harm in someone doing it in voluntary prayers, if he has been standing for a long time, in order to make things easier for himself.'[20] The phrase used, *lā aʿrifu dhālika fī l-farīḍa*, clearly indicates a lack of existential knowledge of this practice. In other words, 'we know about the *ḥadīth*s on this subject, but this is not the way the people are doing, or have done, the prayer here in Medina'. We are reminded of the reports mentioned above, about transmitting a *ḥadīth* 'so that it be known that it is with full knowledge of it that we do not act upon it'. Put differently, it is *sadl*, not *qabḍ*, that is the ongoing *ʿamal* of the people of Medina and thus the judgement to be followed. And this is, indeed, the understanding of the traditional scholars of the *madhhab*, who confirm, first, in a general sense, that not every *ḥadīth* is to be acted upon, even though it may be completely authentic; and, second, in this specific instance, that *sadl* is the *ʿamal* of the people of Medina. Thus, for instance, Muḥammad Ḥabīballāh ibn Māyaʾbā al-Shinqīṭī (d. 1364/1944) says in his *Iḍāʾat al-ḥālik*,

> Not everything that is authentic is acted upon
> Since abrogation may have occurred in its respect.
> It is for this reason that Mālik chose not to act by
> A small number [of reports] in the *Muwaṭṭa*ʾ.
> I say: an example of this is the *ḥadīth* about *qabḍ*,
> Which is abrogated by *sadl* in a manner which is pleasing.[21]

Elsewhere he says, when mentioning that the *ḥadīths* in the *Muwaṭṭa*ʾ are to be understood in the light of reports in the *Mudawwana*, and that Ibn al-Qāsim's transmissions from Mālik are to be given preference over those of other students of the Imam,

> An example of this is the *ḥadīth* about *qabḍ*,
>
> Which is [related] in it (i.e. the *Muwaṭṭaʾ*) with a well-known, faultless *isnād*.
>
> Ibn al-Qāsim restricts the judgement to voluntary prayers
>
> As has come down to us in transmissions from him.
>
> In obligatory prayers it is disliked, as is clear[ly transmitted]
>
> From Mālik, and that is the view that is to be given preference.[22]

He adds, in his commentary on the phrase 'to be given preference', 'in the opinion of Mālik and the majority of the scholars of his *madhhab* … because of the strength of the evidence for it, and the continued practice of it (*jarayān al-ʿamal bihi*) both in the early period in Medina and elsewhere, and more recently in other places'.[23]

On a similar note, Shaykh ʿIllīsh says in his *Fatḥ al-ʿAlī al-Mālik*, in response to a question about whether *qabḍ* is disliked in obligatory prayers whatever the situation (*muṭlaqan*), or just if it is done without the intention of following the *sunna*,

> Ibn al-Qāsim's transmission from Mālik in the *Mudawwana*, which is given precedence over others, is that *qabḍ* is disliked in obligatory prayers, whatever the situation, because it has been abrogated … The text of the *Mudawwana* is: 'Mālik disliked putting the right hand over the left in obligatory prayers, saying "I do not know about this with regard to obligatory prayers", and the meaning of this phrase is, "I do not know about this as the continued practice of the Companions, the Successors, and the Successors of the Successors with regard to obligatory prayers. What I know of as their continued practice with regard to obligatory prayers is *sadl*"'.[24]

These are but three examples: many more could be chosen, such as those chapters relating to inheritance where Mālik specifies the *ʿamal* on a given topic at the beginning of the chapter and then ties it in with the relevant Qur'anic verse at the end of the chapter, or the sections on business transactions which effectively record the Medinans' living response to the Qur'anic prohibition of usury. Nevertheless, they illustrate how *ʿamal* could not only clarify ambiguities in the texts themselves but also be used to add further details and fill out gaps not necessarily obvious from the texts by themselves.

Thus, the *ʿamal* of the people of Medina can act as a *tafsīr* of Qur'an, and a *sharḥ* of *ḥadīth*, but one in which the non-textual has distinct preference over the textual. At the same time, it provides a fuller historical framework for the Qur'an and the *sunna* than that which is simply provided by the texts themselves.

ʿIyāḍ records the following exchange between Mālik and Abū Yūsuf, the Kufan jurist and major student of Abū Ḥanīfa:

> Abū Yūsuf said [to Mālik], 'You do the *adhān* with *tarjīʿ* [repeating the initial phrases of the *adhān* out loud after having said them quietly] but you have no *ḥadīth* from the Prophet about this.' Mālik turned to him and said, '*Subḥāna-llāh* ("Glory be to God")! I have never seen anything more amazing than this! The call to prayer has been done [here] every day in front of witnesses, and sons have inherited it from their fathers, since the time of the Messenger of Allah, may Allah bless him and grant him peace. Does this need "So-and-so from so-and-so"? This is more accurate in our opinion than *ḥadīth*.'
>
> Abū Yūsuf also asked him about the *ṣāʿ* [a measure of volume relating to various judgements of *fiqh*] and Mālik said, 'Five and one-third *raṭls*.' Abū Yūsuf said, 'What's your basis for saying that?' Mālik said to some of the people with him, 'Go and fetch the *ṣāʿ*s that you have.' Many of the people of Medina, [from families of] both the Muhājirūn and the Anṣār, came, and every one of them brought a *ṣāʿ* [with him] and said, 'This is the *ṣāʿ* which I inherited from my father, who inherited it from his father, who was one of the Companions of the Messenger of Allah, may Allah bless him and grant him peace.' Mālik said, 'This sort of widespread knowledge is more reliable in our opinion than *ḥadīth*.' So Abū Yūsuf accepted Mālik's opinion.[25]

In other words, there is another type of transmission of the *sunna* which is not based on *ḥadīth* but, rather, on *ʿamal*. Indeed, as we have seen – in the case of *sadl v. qabḍ* in particular, but also in the exchange above with Abū Yūsuf – this is seen to be stronger than *ḥadīth*, that is, a better indication of the *sunna* than *ḥadīth*.

This distinction between *sunna* as action and *ḥadīth* as words – albeit words about an action – is the main area of dispute between the scholars of Medina, represented by Mālik, and the scholars of the other centres of learning, represented by Abū Ḥanīfa (Kufa, Iraq) and al-Shāfiʿī (Egypt), and others who did not accept the Medinan method of arriving at judgements by *ʿamal*.

It is to some examples of this dispute – which occurs in both ancient and modern forms – that we now turn.

5

Controversies, ancient and modern

In the previous chapter, we noted Qadi ʿIyāḍ's comment that 'all the leaders of the *madhhab*s, whether legal scholars, or theologians, or people of *ḥadīth*, or people of intellectual reasoning, are as one group against us regarding this matter', that is, regarding the validity of Medinan *ʿamal* as a source of law. This opposition manifested most evidently in the different parties' attitude towards *sunna* and how it might or might not be manifested in *ḥadīth* (particularly, but not exclusively, Prophetic *ḥadīth*). We saw also, in the section from ʿIyāḍ's *Madārik* about the *ʿamal* of the people of Medina being a conclusive proof even if it is contrary to *ḥadīth*, that, for Mālik, *ʿamal* was a stronger proof than simply *ḥadīth*, since it represented a continuous and acted-upon tradition from the time of the Prophet and his Companions up until his own time, such as was the case for the size of the *ṣāʿ* and the *mudd*, or the way of calling the *adhān* in Medina, which Mālik described as being 'more accurate than *ḥadīth*'.

We also referred (see Chapter 4) to the two groups of the Medinans and the Kufans as the forerunners of the Mālikī and Ḥanafī *madhhab*s, respectively, and who were soon to become joined by another, third, *madhhab*, that of Imam al-Shāfiʿī.

In this chapter we look at a number of specific examples of disagreement raised by opponents of Mālik and his method in their specialist literature on the subject. Although we have only chosen a few, they give a good idea of the basic issues at stake.

Mālik and al-Shaybānī

Example 1: Passing in front of someone who is doing the prayer

In the *Muwaṭṭa'*, Mālik includes the following two chapters, which appear one after the other:

A. The strong warning against passing in front of someone who is doing the prayer

1. Yaḥyā related to me from Mālik, from Zayd ibn Aslam, from ʿAbd al-Raḥmān ibn Abī Saʿīd al-Khudrī, from his father, that the Messenger of Allah, may Allah bless him and grant him peace, said: 'Don't let anyone pass in front of you when you are doing the prayer. Ward him off as much as you can, and if he refuses, fight him, for he is just a devil.'

2. He told me, from Mālik, from Abū l-Naḍr the mawlā of ʿUmar ibn ʿUbaydallāh, from Busr ibn Saʿīd, that Zayd ibn Khālid al-Juhanī sent him to Abū Juhaym to ask him what he had heard from the Messenger of Allah, may Allah bless him and grant him peace, about someone passing in front of someone doing the prayer. Abū Juhaym said: the Messenger of Allah, may Allah bless him and grant him peace, said: 'If the one passing in front of someone who is doing the prayer knew what he was bringing on himself, it would be better for him to wait forty than to pass in front of him.' Abū l-Naḍr said: 'I don't know if he said "forty days", or "forty months" or "forty years".'

3. He told me, from Mālik, from Zayd ibn Aslam, from ʿAṭā' ibn Yasār, that Kaʿb al-Aḥbār said: 'If the one passing in front of someone who is doing the prayer knew what he was bringing on himself, it would be better for him to sink into the ground than to pass in front of him.'

4. He told me, from Mālik, that he had heard that ʿAbdallāh ibn ʿUmar would dislike passing in front of women while they were doing the prayer.

5. He told me, from Mālik, from Nāfiʿ, that ʿAbdallāh ibn ʿUmar would never pass in front of anyone who was doing the prayer nor would he let anyone pass in front of him.

B. Permission to pass in front of someone who is doing the prayer

1. Yaḥyā told me, from Mālik, from Ibn Shihāb, from ʿUbaydallāh ibn ʿAbdallāh ibn ʿUtba ibn Masʿūd, that ʿAbdallāh ibn ʿAbbās said: 'I came

up riding on a donkey while the Messenger of Allah, may Allah bless him and grant him peace, was leading the people in prayer at Minā, and I was at the time nearing puberty. I passed in front of part of the row, and then dismounted and sent the donkey off to graze, and then joined the row, and no-one rebuked me for what I had done.'

2a. He told me, from Mālik, that he had heard that Sa'd ibn Abī Waqqāṣ would pass in front of some of the rows while the prayer was in progress.

2b. Mālik said: 'I think there is leeway with regard to this, if the *iqāma* has been made and the imam has started the prayer and a man cannot find any way into the mosque except by going between the rows.'

3. He told me, from Mālik, that he had heard that 'Alī ibn Abī Ṭālib said: 'A man's prayer is not broken by anything that passes in front of him.'

4. He told me, from Mālik, from Ibn Shihāb, from Sālim ibn 'Abdallāh, that 'Abdallāh ibn 'Umar used to say: 'A man's prayer is not broken by anything that passes in front him.'[1]

This, then, is what Mālik includes in the two sections that deal with this issue, according to Yaḥyā's transmission from him. (They occur in almost identical form in the transmission of al-Zuhrī, except that Mālik's comment in B2b finishes at the words 'if the *iqāma* has been made'.)[2] It is clear from the two headings that there is effectively a general rule to which there is a possible exception.

Let us compare this presentation with that of al-Shaybānī, in his transmission of the *Muwaṭṭa'* and also in his *al-Ḥujja 'ala ahl al-Madīna* ('The Proof Against the People of Medina').

Al-Shaybānī's transmission of the *Muwaṭṭa'* contains the following chapter – and the reader should not be surprised if it is remarkably similar to what we have just mentioned:

Chapter on someone passing in front of (someone doing) the prayer

1. Mālik informed us: Sālim Abū l-Naḍr the *mawlā* of 'Umar told us, that Busr ibn Sa'īd informed him that Zayd ibn Khālid al-Juhanī sent him to Abū Juhaym al-Anṣārī to ask him what he had heard the Messenger of Allah, may Allah bless him and grant him peace, say about someone passing in front of someone doing the prayer. He said: the Messenger of Allah, may Allah bless him and grant him peace, said: 'If the one passing in front of someone who

is doing the prayer knew what he was bringing on himself, it would be better for him to wait forty than to pass in front of him.' He said: 'I don't know if he said "forty days", or "forty months" or "forty years".' [= report A2 above]

2. Mālik informed us: Zayd ibn Aslam told us, from ʿAbd al-Raḥmān ibn Abī Saʿīd al-Khudrī, from his father, that the Messenger of Allah, may Allah bless him and grant him peace, said: 'Don't let anyone pass in front of you when you are doing the prayer. If he refuses, fight him, for he is just a devil.' [= report A1 above]

3. Mālik informed us: Zayd ibn Aslam told us, from ʿAṭāʾ ibn Yasār, that Kaʿb said: 'If the one passing in front of someone who is doing the prayer knew what he was bringing on himself, it would be better for him to sink into the ground than to pass in front of him.' [= report A3 above]

Muḥammad [ibn al-Ḥasan al-Shaybānī] said: It is disliked for a man to pass in front of someone who is doing the prayer. If someone wants to pass in front of him, he should ward him off as best he can but not fight him. If he fights him, the fighting that he is involved in while doing the prayer is more serious for him than the man passing in front of him. We don't know of anyone who is of the opinion that he should fight him, except what has been related from Abū Saʿīd al-Khudrī. The majority do not follow this, but, rather, what I have described to you, and this is Abū Ḥanīfa's opinion.

4. Mālik informed us: al-Zuhrī told us, from Sālim ibn ʿAbdallāh, that Ibn ʿUmar said: 'The prayer is not broken by anything.' [see report B4 above]

Muḥammad said: 'This is what we go by. The prayer is not broken by anything that passes in front of someone who is doing the prayer.'[3]

Once again, as we saw in Chapter 3, al-Shaybānī's transmission, while maintaining the textual integrity of the reports he transmits – with some very small differences, such as in the names '**Sālim** Abū l-Naḍr the *mawlā* of ʿUmar' rather than 'Abū l-Naḍr the *mawlā* of ʿUmar **ibn ʿUbaydallāh**', and 'Kaʿb' rather than 'Kaʿb **al-Aḥbār**' – chooses to exclude certain reports that do not reflect his position and that of Abū Ḥanīfa, as he also adds comments that clarify his and Abū Ḥanīfa's position.

In his book *Kitāb al-Ḥujja ʿala ahl al-Madīna*, al-Shaybānī deals at some length with this issue.[4] He says,

Abū Ḥanīfa said: It is not correct for a man to pass in front of someone who is doing the prayer, regardless of whether it is a voluntary or obligatory [prayer] or whether the *iqāma* has been made and people have started doing the prayer. If someone does pass in front of someone who is doing the prayer, he should ward him off as best he can. If he refuses, so that he would have to fight him, he should let the man pass by without fighting him, for fighting whilst doing the prayer is more serious than having the man pass in front of him.

The people of Medina say, about someone passing in front of people while they are doing the prayer: 'We think there is leeway with regard to this, if the *iqāma* has been made.' [cf. report B2b]

Muḥammad ibn al-Ḥasan said: The reports about not passing in front of people while they are doing the prayer, [both] after the *iqāma* and before the *iqāma*, are too numerous for us to go by the opinion of one who says, 'There is no harm in this, if the *iqāma* has been made.'

The people of Medina say: 'But we have heard that Saʿd ibn Abī Waqqāṣ would pass in front of people while they were doing the prayer.' [= report B2a above].

Our reply is: 'This has been related from Mālik ibn Anas, from Saʿd, without him mentioning any *isnād* or naming any source. Rather he just says, "We have heard that Saʿd would do this." '[5]

Al-Shaybānī then quotes exactly the same *ḥadīth*s that he transmits in his version of the *Muwaṭṭa*ʾ, namely reports A1, A2 and A3 above, except that he adds, after report A1, the words 'Mālik then says that "fighting him" means "pushing him away"', and also includes Ibn ʿUmar's report (A5) between reports A1 and A2. He then concludes,

So these are the *ḥadīth*s of the people of Medina which are an argument against them and which they go against (*yaʾkhudhūna bi-khilāfihā*), and one of the ones who goes against them is Mālik ibn Anas, although he is the one who relates them. How can they be people of reports when they openly leave aside what they have related? If we wanted to argue against them using many other *ḥadīth*s on this and related points, we could do so, but using their own *ḥadīth*s provides a stronger argument against them. This also points to how, in other opinions of theirs, they leave reports aside and go by what they think is good (*bi-mā istaḥsanū*), without them backing it up by any report (*athar*) or *sunna*.[6]

Al-Shaybānī's criticism is thus clear: Mālik and the Medinans claim to go by reports (*āthār*) but do so inconsistently, allowing exceptions to general rules with only the authority of a single Companion (in this case, Saʿd ibn Abī Waqqāṣ), and in a report which doesn't even have a full *isnād* to it, rather than accepting the overriding authority of the Prophet in fully backed-up *ḥadīth*s.

What is also noticeable, though, is the textual consistency between these sources. It is clear that al-Shaybānī is relying on exactly the same reports, even if his overall interpretation is different.

Example 2: *Zakāt* on mines

In the *Muwaṭṭaʾ*, Mālik includes the following two chapters, sequentially, in the Book of *Zakāt*:

A. Zakāt *on mines*

1a. Yaḥyā told me, from Mālik, from Rabīʿa ibn Abī ʿAbd al-Raḥmān, from more than one person, that the Messenger of Allah, may Allah bless him and grant him peace, assigned the mines of al-Qabaliyya, which lie in the direction of al-Furʿ [a place between Mecca and Medina], to Bilāl ibn al-Ḥārith al-Muzanī, and up until this day only *zakāt* has ever been taken from these mines.

1b. Mālik said: 'I think, and Allah knows best, that nothing should be taken from what is extracted from mines until what is extracted from them reaches an amount of twenty dinars of gold or two hundred dirhams [of silver]. When it reaches that amount, *zakāt* should be taken from it, there and then. If the amount comes to more than that, [*zakāt*] is taken from it accordingly, for as long as the mine is producing. If the vein runs out but then, later, more is obtained from [the mine], the new supply is dealt with in the same way as the first, and *zakāt* starts to be taken from it as it was from the first.'

1c. Mālik said: 'Mines are treated the same way as agricultural produce. [*Zakāt*] is taken from them in the same way that it is taken from agricultural produce: it is taken from what the mine has produced on the day that it is produced, without waiting for a year to elapse, in the same way that a tenth is taken from agricultural produce on the day that it is harvested, without waiting for a year to elapse.'

B. Zakāt *on buried treasure (*rikāz*)*

1a. Yaḥyā told me, from Mālik, from Ibn Shihāb, from Saʿīd ibn al-Musayyab and Abū Salama ibn ʿAbd al-Raḥmān, from Abū Hurayra, that the Messenger of Allah, may Allah bless him and grant him peace, said: 'A fifth [is due] on buried treasure (*rikāz*).'

1b. Mālik said: 'The position on which there is no disagreement here with us, and which I have heard the people of knowledge mentioning, is that *rikāz* refers to treasure that is found that was buried in the time of the Jāhiliyya, without needing any capital, or expense, or a lot of work and effort [to recover]. If it needs capital, or a lot of work, with success on one occasion and failure on another, it is not *rikāz*.'[7]

Elsewhere, in the 'General section on blood-money', Mālik includes a longer version of Abū Hurayra's *ḥadīth* (i.e. report B1a above):

[C1] Yaḥyā told me, from Mālik, from Ibn Shihāb, from Sa'īd ibn al-Musayyab and Abū Salama ibn 'Abd al-Raḥmān, from Abū Hurayra, that the Messenger of Allah, may Allah bless him and grant him peace, said: 'An animal is free of liability (*jubār*) if it causes an injury; a well is free of liability [if someone falls into it]; a mine is free of liability [if it collapses on someone];[8] and a fifth is due on *rikāz*.'

Mālik said: 'The meaning (*tafsīr*) of the word *jubār* is that there is no compensation (*diya*) to be paid [for any injury caused].'

Mālik said: '[Regardless of] whether someone is leading an animal, or driving it, or riding it, he is liable for what that animal [treads on and] destroys, except if the animal has bolted without anything having been done to make it bolt. 'Umar gave the judgement that blood-money had to be paid in the case of the man who made his horse run.'[9]

Al-Shaybānī, in his transmission of the *Muwaṭṭa'*, combines these reports into the following section:

Chapter on Rikāz

Mālik informed us: Rabī'a ibn Abī 'Abd al-Raḥmān and others told us, that the Messenger of Allah, may Allah bless him and grant him peace, assigned some mines from among the mines of al-Qabaliyya, which is in the direction of al-Fur', to Bilāl ibn al-Ḥārith al-Muzanī, and, up until this day, only *zakāt* has been taken from these mines. [= report A1 above].

Muḥammad [ibn al-Ḥasan al-Shaybānī] said: 'There is the well-known *ḥadīth* that the Prophet, may Allah bless him and grant him peace, said: "A fifth [is due] on buried treasure (*rikāz*)." Someone said, "O Messenger of

> Allah, what is *rikāz*?" He said: "Wealth that Allah created in the earth on the day He created the heavens and the earth." So a fifth is due on mines such as these, and that is the opinion of Abū Ḥanīfa and the majority of our jurists.'[10]

Elsewhere, in the section dealing with blood money, al-Shaybānī also includes the same *ḥadīth* as above (report C1) about wells and then says,

> This is what we go by. '*Jubār*' means liability-free. 'An animal' here refers to one that has run loose and then wounded or injured somebody. 'A well' and 'a mine' refers to when a man hires someone to dig a well or a mine and it falls on him and kills him. There is no liability for that. 'And a fifth is due on *rikāz*: '*rikāz* refers to whatever is taken out of a mine, whether it be gold, silver, lead, copper, iron, or mercury: a fifth is due on it. This is the opinion of Abū Ḥanīfa and the majority of our jurists.
>
> Mālik informed us: Ibn Shihāb told us, from Ḥizām ibn Sa'd ibn Muḥayyiṣa, that a camel belonging to al-Barā' ibn 'Āzib went into someone's orchard and caused a lot of damage. The Messenger of Allah, may Allah bless him and grant him peace, gave the judgement (*qaḍā*) that it was the responsibility of the owners of orchards to protect them during the day, but that whatever damage was done by livestock during the night was the responsibility of the owners of the livestock.[11]

Al-Shaybānī takes up the issue in his *Kitāb al-Ḥujja*:

Gold and silver that is extracted from mines

> Abū Ḥanīfa said that a fifth is taken from gold and silver that is extracted from mines, whether it is a little or a lot.
>
> The people of Medina say: 'Nothing should be taken from what is extracted from mines until what is extracted from them reaches an amount of twenty dinars of gold or two hundred dirhams [of silver]. When it reaches that amount, *zakāt* should be taken from it, there and then. If the amount comes to more than that, [*zakāt*] is taken from it accordingly, for as long as the mine is producing. If the vein runs out but then, later, more is obtained from [the mine], the new supply is dealt with in the same way as the first, and *zakāt* starts to be taken from it as it was from the first.' [= report B1b above].
>
> Muḥammad ibn al-Ḥasan [al-Shaybānī] said: '*Zakāt* does not apply to mines. Rather, mines are like booty, on which a fifth is due, whether [it is] a little or a lot. We have heard that the Messenger of Allah, may Allah bless him and grant him peace, said: "A fifth [is due] on buried treasure (*rikāz*)." Someone said, "O Messenger of Allah, what is *rikāz*?" He said: "Wealth that

Allah created in the earth on the day He created the heavens and the earth." So a fifth is due on such mines.'

The people of Medina say that *rikāz* refers to wealth that was buried in the time of the Jāhiliyya, which does not need any capital, or expense, or a lot of work [to recover]. If it needs capital, or a lot of work, with success on one occasion and failure on another, it is not *rikāz*. [= report B1b above]

Abū Ḥanīfa said: 'This and [wealth from] mines is the same. Whether it needs a lot of work [to extract] or whether it has been found without any effort, it is the same: on this, and what is extracted from mines, a fifth is due.'

Muḥammad ibn al-Ḥasan said: '*Rikāz* is what is found in mines, and buried treasure is considered the same as wealth that is extracted from mines. This is a matter of the Arabic language that I would not have thought the people of Medina would have held a contrary opinion about. One says, *arkaza al-maʿdin* ("the mine produced *rikāz*"), meaning that a lot of wealth was extracted from it. There is [also] the well-known *ḥadīth* that a man asked the Messenger of Allah, may Allah bless him and grant him peace, "What do you say about [wealth] that is found in a village that is no longer lived in?" He said, may Allah bless him and grant him peace, "On it, and on *rikāz*, a fifth is due", thus considering it to be of a different category to *rikāz*.'

Al-Shaybānī then mentions a long *ḥadīth* about various types of lost property, which also contains the phrase 'a fifth is due on *rikāz*'. He then cites another version of the '*jubār*' *ḥadīth*, from Abū Ḥanīfa, also containing the phrase 'and a fifth is due on *rikāz*', and then closes the chapter by citing a report from ʿAlī about a fifth being due on some buried treasure that was found 'in one of the buildings of the non-Arabs'.[12]

So, whereas the Medinans consider gold and silver produced from mines to be subject to *zakāt*, Abū Ḥanīfa and those following him consider anything precious that is taken out of the ground to be subject to the tax of one-fifth, without differentiating between what has involved effort and what hasn't.

Mālik, al-Shaybānī and al-Shāfiʿī

Example 3: The purity of water that a dog has licked

In the *Muwaṭṭaʾ*, Mālik includes the following *ḥadīth*, in the 'General chapter on *wuḍūʾ*':

A1. [Yaḥyā] told me, from Mālik, from Abū l-Zinād, from al-Aʿraj, from Abū Hurayra, that the Messenger of Allah, may Allah bless him and grant him peace, said: 'If a dog drinks from a vessel of yours, you should wash it seven times.'[13]

He also includes, in the chapter on 'Pure water for doing *wuḍūʾ*', two other *ḥadīth*s about water that animals have drunk from:

B1a. [Yaḥyā] told me, from Mālik, from Isḥāq ibn ʿAbdallāh ibn Abī Ṭalḥa, from Ḥumayda, the daughter of ʿUbayda ibn Farwa, from her maternal aunt Kabsha, the daughter of Kaʿb ibn Mālik – who was married to Abū Qatāda al-Anṣārī – that she had told her that Abū Qatāda came in [one day] and she poured out some water for him to do *wuḍūʾ* with. A cat came to drink from it and he tilted the vessel so that [the cat] could drink from it. Kabsha said, 'He saw me looking at him, and said, "Are you surprised, my cousin?" I said, "Yes". He said, "The Messenger of Allah, may Allah bless him and grant him peace, said, 'They are not impure. They are part of your household that come and go around you.' " '

B1b. Mālik said: There is no harm in [such water] as long as you do not see any impurity on [the cat's] mouth.

B2. [Yaḥyā] told me, from Mālik, from Yaḥyā ibn Saʿīd, from Muḥammad ibn Ibrāhīm ibn al-Ḥārith al-Taymī, from Yaḥyā ibn ʿAbd al-Raḥmān ibn Ḥāṭib, that ʿUmar was once on a journey with a group of people, among whom was ʿAmr ibn al-ʿĀṣī. They came to a pool, and ʿAmr ibn al-ʿĀṣī said to the owner, 'O owner of the pool! Do wild beasts come and drink from this pool?' ʿUmar ibn al-Khaṭṭāb said, 'O owner of the pool, do not tell us. We come and drink after the wild beasts and they come and drink after us.'[14]

Al-Shaybānī, in his transmission, does not include the *ḥadīth* about dogs, but he does include the one about cats, which he includes in the chapter on 'Doing *wuḍūʾ* with water a cat has drunk from', after which he says, 'There is no harm in doing *wuḍūʾ* with water left over after a cat has drunk from it, although to use other water is preferable in our opinion. This is [also] the view of Abū Ḥanīfa.'[15]

Al-Shaybānī also includes the *ḥadīth* about wild beasts, in the chapter on 'Doing *wuḍūʾ* with water that wild beasts have drunk from or licked', after which he adds the comment:

If the pool is large, such that if you move the water on one side, the water on the other side doesn't move, that water is not harmed by any wild animal that drinks from it, nor by anything dirty that falls into it, unless it changes the smell or taste. If the pool is small, such that if you move the water on one side, the water on the other side moves, and wild beasts drink from it, or something dirty falls into it, it should not be used for doing *wuḍūʾ*. Do you not see that ʿUmar ibn al-Khaṭṭāb disliked [the man] telling him, and told him not to do so?[16]

In the *Mudawwana*, we find the following chapter about the subject, presented in the form of an exchange between Saḥnūn ('I said') and Ibn al-Qāsim ('He said'):

Doing wuḍūʾ *with water that animals, chickens and dogs have drunk from*

[Ibn al-Qāsim] said: 'I asked Mālik about water that donkeys and mules have drunk from, and he said, "There is no harm in it".'

I [i.e. Saḥnūn] said: 'What would you think if it gets onto something else?' He said, 'It and that something else are the same (*huwa wa-ghayruhu sawāʾ*).'

He said: 'There is no harm in the sweat of pack-horses, mules and donkeys.'

He said: 'Mālik said, about a vessel that has water in it that a dog has drunk from: "If he has used it to do *wuḍūʾ* and has then done the prayer, that is acceptable." '

He said: 'He did not consider dogs to be like other [animals].'

He said: 'Mālik said: "If a bird or animal that eats carrion drinks from a vessel, that water should not be used for doing *wuḍūʾ*." '

He said: 'Mālik said: "If a dog drinks from a vessel that has milk (*laban*) in it, there is no harm in consuming that milk.' "

I said: 'Did Mālik say that a vessel should be washed seven times if a dog has drunk from it, if it contains milk or water?'

He said: 'Mālik said: "There is the *ḥadīth* that has been transmitted [about this], but I do not know what its real meaning (*ḥaqīqa*) is." '

He said: 'It is as if he considered dogs to be part of the household, and not like other wild beasts. He would say, "If a vessel is to be washed, it should only be when it has had water in it", although he still considered this a weak opinion.

He added: "It should not be washed if it has had fat (*samn*) or milk in it, and anything like this that a dog has licked can be eaten. I consider it a serious matter that someone should go to any provision that Allah has provided [people] with and then throw it away because a dog has licked it."'

I said: 'If a bird or an animal that eats carrion, or a chicken that eats filth (*natin*), drinks from the milk, can the milk be consumed or not?'

He said: 'If you are certain that it has some dirt on its beak, you shouldn't drink [the milk], but if you don't see anything on its beak, then there is no harm in it. It is not like water, because water can be thrown away and not used for *wuḍū'*.'

Ibn Wahb [relates], from ʿAmr ibn al-Ḥārith, that Yaḥyā ibn Saʿīd and Bukayr ibn ʿAbdallāh would both say that there is no harm in a man doing *wuḍū'* with water that donkeys or mules or other animals have drunk from. Ibn Shihāb said the same about donkeys.

Ibn Wahb [relates that] ʿAṭā' ibn Abī Rabāḥ, Rabīʿa, and Abū l-Zinād said the same about donkeys and mules, and ʿAṭā' recited the words of Allah, the Blessed and Exalted, 'Horses, mules and donkeys, for you to ride and as an adornment' [Q.16:8]. Mālik said the same, according to a report from Ibn Wahb.

ʿAlī ibn Ziyād [relates], that Mālik said, about someone who does *wudu'* with water that a dog has drunk from and then does the prayer, 'I do not consider that he has to repeat the prayer, even if he learns about the situation within the time for the prayer.'

ʿAlī [ibn Ziyād] and Ibn Wahb [relate], that Mālik said: 'I do not like [people] doing *wuḍū'* with water that a dog has drunk from, if it is only a small amount of water; but there is no harm in doing so if it is a large amount of water, such as a pool with a large amount of water in it, or anything else of that nature.'

Ibn Wahb [relates], from Ibn Jurayj, that the Messenger of Allah, may Allah bless him and grant him peace, came down to a waterhole with Abū Bakr and ʿUmar. The people in charge of the water came out and said, 'O Messenger of Allah, wild beasts and dogs drink from this pool.' He said: 'For them is what they have taken into their stomachs, and for us is what is left – a drink which is pure and purifying.'

ʿAbd al-Raḥmān ibn Zayd told me the same, from Zayd ibn Aslam, from ʿAṭā' ibn Yasār, from Abū Hurayra, from the Messenger of Allah, may Allah bless him and grant him peace. ʿUmar also said, 'Do not tell us, O owner of the pool. We drink after the wild beasts and they drink after us.' Dogs are less problematic than wild beasts, and cats are even less so, because they are [animals] that people keep [in their houses].

Ibn al-Qāsim said: 'Mālik said: "There is no harm if the saliva of a dog gets onto a man's clothing." Rabīʿa said the same. Ibn Shihāb said: "There is no harm if you are forced to use water that a dog has drunk from to do *wuḍūʾ* with." Mālik said: "One eats game that it has hunted, so how can its saliva be disliked?"'[17]

Mālik is therefore clearly of the opinion that food, in particular, should not be wasted just because a dog has licked it. He is well aware of the *ḥadīth* about washing a vessel seven times if a dog has drunk water from it – he himself relates it in the *Muwaṭṭaʾ* – but he reserves judgement as to its 'reality' (*ḥaqīqa*); that is, he is not sure of the full implications of the words: what applies to water need not necessarily apply to milk, or gravy, or any other liquid; and what applies to dogs need not necessarily apply to other animals, or birds, and, indeed, need not necessarily apply in all circumstances.

Let us now consider, by comparison, al-Shāfiʿī's view of the same issue as discussed in his *Kitāb al-Umm*, in the section on the differences of opinion between him and Mālik (*Kitāb Ikhtilāf Mālik wa-l-Shāfiʿī*):

Dogs drinking out of a vessel or anything else

I [i.e. al-Rabīʿ ibn Sulayman] asked al-Shāfiʿī about a dog drinking from a vessel in which there is an amount of less than two large jars (*qullatayn*) of water, or milk, or gravy.

He said: 'The water, milk, or gravy should be thrown away and not used, and the vessel should be washed seven times. Any [part of a] garment that that water or milk gets onto, must be washed, because that [water or milk] is impure.'

I said: 'What is the argument for that?'

He said: 'Mālik informed us, from Abū l-Zinād, from al-Aʿraj, from Abū Hurayra, that the Messenger of Allah, may Allah bless him and grant him peace, said: "If a dog drinks from a vessel of yours, you should wash it seven times."'

Al-Shāfiʿī said: 'It is thus clear in the *sunna* of the Messenger of Allah, may Allah bless him and grant him peace, [that], if a dog drinks water from a vessel and the vessel becomes impure so that it needs to be washed seven times, it has become impure because of the water that has come into contact with it. The water is more susceptible (*awlā*) of becoming impure than the vessel, which has only become impure because the water has touched it. And if water – which is pure and purifying (*ṭahūr*) – becomes impure [in such a way], then milk and gravy, which are not pure and purifying – are even more susceptible to becoming impure by whatever makes the water impure.'[18]

It is thus clear that al-Shāfiʿī is not willing to entertain any exceptions to what he considers a general rule. The *ḥadīth* in his view clearly indicates the impurity of what dogs have licked, and so there is only one conclusion: any liquid they lick becomes impure and the vessel containing it becomes impure and needs to be washed seven times before it can be considered pure again.

For Mālik, however, things are not so clear-cut, and there is counter-evidence. In particular, dogs are used for hunting, by Quranic and Prophetic authority, and if one is allowed to eat what they have sunk their teeth into, and thus mixed their saliva with, then it cannot be that everything a dog's saliva touches becomes impure. As he says, 'One eats game that it has hunted, so how can its saliva be disliked?' Furthermore, given the existence of this kind of counter-evidence, he considers it a serious matter to throw away food that Allah has provided people with simply because a dog has licked it. And so it is that he recognizes the existence of the *ḥadīth* but does not know what its 'reality' is.

Example 4: Bringing 'dead' land (*al-mawāt*) to life

Mālik includes the following chapter in the *Muwaṭṭa*ʾ:

The judgement about developing 'dead' land

1a. Yaḥyā related to me, from Mālik, from Hishām ibn ʿUrwa, from his father, that the Messenger of Allah, may Allah bless him and grant him peace, said: 'If anyone brings "dead" land to life, it is his, and an unjust root has no right.'

1b. Mālik said: 'An "unjust root" refers to whatever is dug, or taken, or planted, without a right.'

2a. Mālik related to me [*sic*], from Ibn Shihāb, from Sālim ibn ʿAbdallāh, from his father, that ʿUmar ibn al-Khaṭṭāb said: 'If anyone brings "dead" land to life, it is his.'

2b. Mālik said: 'That is the position here with us.'[19]

The same two *ḥadīth*s are related from the same sources in the transmission of al-Shaybānī, in a chapter entitled 'Bringing "dead" land to life, whether with the permission of the imam or not', where al-Shaybānī adds the following comment:

> We go by this, that if anyone brings 'dead' land to life, with or without the permission of the imam, it is his. Abū Ḥanīfa said: 'It is not his unless the imam confirms that it is his.' He also said: 'The imam should confirm that it is his, if he has brought it to life; if he doesn't do so, it is not his.'[20]

In the *Mudawwana*, we are given more details about this distinction. In the relevant section on 'What has come down about bringing "dead" land to life', we find the following passage:

> I [Saḥnūn] said: 'What do you think about someone who brings "dead" land to life without the permission (*amr*) of the imam? Is it his, or is it not his until the imam has given him permission, according to Mālik?'
>
> He [Ibn al-Qāsim] said: 'Mālik said: "If he brings it to life, it is his, even if he hasn't sought permission from the imam." Mālik said: "Bringing it to life means creating watercourses, digging wells, planting trees, building buildings, and planting crops. If he does any of these, he has brought it to life." He added: "He should not do this where it is near to settled land. The explanation (*tafsīr*) of the *ḥadīth*, 'If anyone brings "dead" land to life, it belongs to him', is that it refers to open land and desert. If it is near to settled land and is [land] that people are naturally covetous about, then he can only bring it to life if it has been allocated to him by the imam." '[21]

We see, therefore, that Mālik draws a distinction between land that is some distance from where people are living, which anyone is free to bring to life, and land which is near to where people are living, which can only be brought to life if the imam has given permission for this to be done. It also seems to be the case, as mentioned in al-Shaybānī's transmission, that Abū Ḥanīfa assumes that the imam's permission is always needed, although al-Shaybānī himself doesn't take this view.

Al-Shāfiʿī, for his part, takes a characteristically straightforward view. In the *Kitāb al-Umm* we read:

I [i.e. al-Rabīʿ ibn Sulaymān] asked al-Shāfiʿī about someone who brings 'dead' land to life, and he said: 'If the "dead" land has no owner and it is brought to life by one of the people of Islam, then it is his and not anyone else's. It doesn't make any difference to me whether the sultan has given it to him or not, because the Prophet, may Allah bless him and grant him peace, has given it to him, and what the Prophet, may Allah bless him and grant him peace, has given [to someone] has more right to be acknowledged as a gift than the gift of the sultan.'

I said: 'What is your argument for saying this?'

He said: '[It is] what has been related by Mālik from the Prophet, may Allah bless him and grant him peace, and one of his Companions.'

Al-Shāfiʿī said: 'Mālik informed us, from Hishām [ibn ʿUrwa], from his father, that the Prophet, may Allah bless him and grant him peace, said, "If anyone brings 'dead' land to life, it is his, and an unjust root has no right." '

Al-Shāfiʿī said: 'Mālik informed us, from Ibn Shihāb, from Sālim [ibn ʿAbdallāh], from his father, that ʿUmar ibn al-Khaṭṭāb said: "If anyone brings 'dead' land to life, it is his." '

Al-Shāfiʿī said: 'Sufyān and others informed us, via a different *isnād* to this, of a report from the Prophet, may Allah bless him and grant him peace, with the same meaning.'

Al-Shāfiʿī said: 'This is what we go by. The gift that the Messenger of Allah, gave the one who brings "dead" land to life, that it is his, is more [of a gift] (*akthar*) to him than the gift of the governor.'

I said to al-Shāfiʿī: 'We dislike someone bringing "dead" land to life unless it is with the permission of the governor.'

Al-Shāfiʿī said, may Allah have mercy on him: 'How is it that you go against what you relate from the Prophet, may Allah bless him and grant him peace, and ʿUmar, when this, in your view, is *sunna*, and ʿ*amal* after them both; and [how] do you affirm the right of the governor to give [something to someone], when it is not the governor's right to give something that is not his, or to withhold from someone something that is his. There is no constraint on someone taking what is his, and, if he has brought "dead" land to life, he has taken what is his, without there being any objection to that, so that someone might say, with regard to that which to which he is fully entitled and which he has a right to take, "Don't take it unless you have the permission of the imam!" If someone were to say [about such a situation] that this is a matter that the sultan must investigate, he would only investigate it if there was another party disputing the case, and if it seems clear in his opinion that [the land] has no owner. If he were to give it to someone, and then the rightful owner were to come and claim it as his, he would give it to the rightful owner. Similarly, if someone were to take [land] and bring it to life without his permission, the sultan has no role in the matter. He would only have a role if, when he gave it to someone, no-one else could claim that it was his and take it from [that other person]. As for someone putting forward a claim to be the rightful owner after the sultan has given it to him, that is meaningless, except in the sense of someone taking what is already his.'

Al-Shāfiʿī said: 'This is an arbitrary approach to knowledge, leaving aside what you have related from the Prophet, may Allah bless him and grant him peace, and ʿUmar, when no-one that we know of among the Companions of the Prophet, may Allah bless him and grant him peace, expressed a contrary view to them, because of an opinion you have, and restricting for others [what should be] broader than this.'

I said to al-Shāfiʿī: 'Have any others taken a contrary opinion to you in this?'

He said: 'I do not know of anyone who has a contrary opinion in this matter, other than yourselves and those you have related this from, other than Abū Ḥanīfa. I think that you have heard his words and gone by them, although Abū Yusuf took a contrary position and held the same view as we do and blamed Abū Ḥanīfa for going against the *sunna*.'

Al-Shāfiʿī, may Allah have mercy on him, said: 'Part of what also contains the same meaning of what you have an opposing view about is what you have related from the Prophet, may Allah bless him and grant him peace, and those after him, with no-one expressing an opposing view, [which is] that Mālik informed us, from ʿAmr ibn Yaḥyā al-Māzinī, from his father, that the Messenger of Allah, may Allah bless him and grant him peace, said: "There [should be] no harm or reciprocal harm."[22] [Mālik] then follows this up, in his book [i.e. the *Muwaṭṭa*ʾ], with [the following] *ḥadīth*, as if he considers it to be an explanation of it.'

Al-Shāfiʿī said: 'Mālik informed us, from Ibn Shihāb, from al-Aʿraj, from Abū Hurayra, that the Messenger of Allah, may Allah bless him and grant him peace, said: "No-one should prevent his neighbour from fixing a wooden peg in his wall." Abū Hurayra then said: "Why is it that I see you turning away from this? By Allah, I will keep on at you about it."'[23]

Al-Shāfiʿī said: 'He then follows this with [the following] two *ḥadīth*s from ʿUmar, as if he considers them to be about the same subject.'

Al-Shāfiʿī, may Allah have mercy on him, said: 'Mālik informed us from ʿAmr ibn Yaḥyā al-Māzinī, from his father, that al-Ḍaḥḥāk ibn Khalīfa dug an irrigation ditch from al-ʿUrayḍ. He wanted it to pass by him via the land of Muḥammad ibn Maslama, but Muḥammad [ibn Maslama] refused. So al-Ḍaḥḥāk spoke to ʿUmar ibn al-Khaṭṭāb about it, and ʿUmar ibn al-Khaṭṭāb called for Muḥammad ibn Maslama and told him to clear the way, but Ibn Maslama said, "No." ʿUmar said, "Why are you stopping your brother from accessing what is of benefit to him and is also useful to you? You drink from it at the beginning and at the end and this doesn't cause you any harm." But Muḥammad said, "No." So ʿUmar said, "By Allah. It will pass by him even if it is over your belly!" '[24]

Al-Shāfiʿī said: 'Mālik informed us, from ʿAmr ibn Yaḥyā al-Māzinī, from his father, that he said, "There was a stream (*rabīʿ*) in my grandfather's garden belonging to ʿAbd al-Raḥmān ibn ʿAwf. ʿAbd al-Raḥmān ibn ʿAwf wanted to change its course to a part of the garden that was nearer to his land, but the owner of the garden wouldn't let him. ʿAbd al-Raḥmān ibn ʿAwf spoke to ʿUmar, and ʿUmar gave judgement that it should pass by him, and this was done." '[25]

Al-Shāfiʿī, may Allah have mercy on him, said: 'So you have related in this book [i.e. the *Muwaṭṭaʾ*] a sound and trustworthy *ḥadīth* from the Prophet, may Allah bless him and grant him peace, and two *ḥadīth*s from ʿUmar ibn al-Khaṭṭāb and then gone against all of them and said about each one, "This is not used for judging between people (*lā yuqḍā bi-hā ʿalā l-nās*)" and "The *ʿamal* is not in accord with them." You have not recorded from any person that I know anything that is contrary to these [reports] or even one of them. So whose *ʿamal* is it that you are referring to by which you go against the *sunna* of the Messenger of Allah, may Allah bless him and grant him peace? It is more fitting in our opinion that this *ʿamal* be rejected. You are going against ʿUmar, as well as the *sunna*. It is problematic to go against just ʿUmar, but to go against the *sunna* as well is even more problematic, but you say you are going by *ʿamal*. We do not know what you mean by *ʿamal*, right up until this day, and I do not think we will ever know for as long as we live.'[26]

Again, as we saw above, al-Shāfiʿī relies on exactly the same reports that Mālik cites, but he puts them into a framework that allows no exceptions to the general rule, and certainly not any exceptions that seem to rely on the amorphous – in his view – concept of *ʿamal*.

Al-Layth ibn Saʿd's letter to Mālik

Al-Layth ibn Saʿd (d. 175/791) was one of Mālik's contemporaries and one of the chief scholars in Egypt in his time. As for his status, it is recorded that Ibn Wahb said of him, 'If it were not for al-Layth and Mālik, we would have gone astray,'[27] while al-Shāfiʿī said, 'Knowledge revolves around three people: Mālik, al-Layth and Sufyān ibn ʿUyayna.'[28] Al-Shāfiʿī even said of al-Layth, when he arrived in Egypt after al-Layth's death, that al-Layth was more knowledgeable than Mālik, but that it was his followers who had let him down after his death.[29]

We have referred (Chapter 4) to Mālik's letter to al-Layth ibn Saʿd on hearing that he was giving *fatwā*s that were contrary to the established position in Medina. Mālik had written to him in the following way:

> From Mālik ibn Anas to al-Layth ibn Saʿd: Peace be upon you. I praise Allah, other than whom there is no god, to you. Know that I have heard that you are giving *fatwā*s to people contrary to that which a group of the Muslims here in this city of ours follow. You, as an imam and a person of excellence and high standing in the eyes of the people of your land, and in view of their need of you and their reliance upon what comes to them from you, should fear for yourself and follow that by which you hope to achieve safety.

He then mentioned some of the special qualities of Medina and of the people who were living there in the first days of Islam, as we have noted above. He then says,

> Know that the only reason I am writing this to you is to give you advice for the sake of Allah, because of my concern for you and my good opinion of you. So consider my letter [to you] in the way it should be considered and, if you do so, you will realize that I have not spared you any good counsel.

He then signs off, making *duʿāʾ* for him, and dating the letter.

Al-Layth's reply

After greeting him, part of al-Layth's reply to Mālik is as follows:

You have heard that I have been giving *fatwās* contrary to that which is followed by a group of people where you are, and that I should fear for myself because of the reliance of the people here on the *fatwās* I give them, and that everyone should follow the people of Medina, which is the place to which the Hijra was made and in which the Qur'an was revealed.

You are right in what you have written, God willing, and I have taken it in the way that you would like. Nor is there anyone to whom knowledge is attributed who is more hateful of irregular judgements (*shawādhdh al-futyā*), nor anyone who gives more preference to the scholars of the people of Medina who have passed away, nor anyone who is more ready to accept their *fatwās* in what they are agreed on than me. Praise be to Allah, the Lord of all the worlds. He has no partner.

As for what you mention about the Messenger of Allah, may Allah bless him and grant him peace, being in Medina, and the Qur'an being revealed to him there while he was among his Companions, and what Allah taught them from him, and how [all] people should follow them with regard to that, it is as you have said.

As for what you say about Allah's word 'The first forerunners among the Muhājirūn and Anṣār, and those who followed them in doing good: Allah is pleased with them and they are pleased with Him. He has prepared gardens for them with rivers flowing under them, remaining in them timelessly, for ever and ever. That is the great victory' [Q.9:100], many of those first forerunners went out on *jihād* for the sake of Allah, seeking the pleasure of Allah. They put together armies, and people gathered to them, and they showed them what was [in] the Book of Allah and the Sunna of His Prophet, without concealing from them anything that they knew. In every army there was a group among them who would teach the Book of Allah and the Sunna of His Prophet and who would exercise their intellect with regard to matters not explained by the Qur'an and the Sunna. Foremost among those who did this were Abū Bakr, ʿUmar and ʿUthmān, whom the Muslims had chosen for themselves. These three did not fall short regarding the armies of the Muslims nor were they unaware of their needs. Rather, they would write to them even about small matters relating to the establishment of the *dīn*, and warn them against differing about the Qur'an and the Sunna of His Prophet. There was no matter that the Qur'an had explained, or that the Prophet had acted by or that they had agreed to act upon after him, without them teaching it to them. If there was a matter that the Companions of the

Messenger of Allah, may Allah bless him and grant him peace, acted upon in Egypt or Syria or Iraq at the time of Abū Bakr, ʿUmar and ʿUthmān, and which they were still doing up until they died, they did not tell them to do anything else. So we do not consider it acceptable for the armies of the Muslims today to introduce anything new that their predecessors (*salaf*) among the Companions of the Messenger of Allah, may Allah bless him and grant him peace, and their Successors had not acted by – although the Companions of the Messenger of Allah, may Allah bless him and grant him peace, did have differences of opinion afterwards, in their *fatwā*s, on many things. If I did not know that you knew these things, I would have written them down for you. Then the Successors had differences of opinion on [many] things after the Companions of the Messenger of Allah, may Allah bless him and grant him peace. [Men such as] Saʿīd ibn al-Musayyab and his like had strong disagreements among themselves, as did those coming after them and who you have known personally in Medina and elsewhere. The chief ones among them at that time were Ibn Shihāb and Rabīʿa ibn Abī ʿAbd al-Raḥmān. Rabīʿa's disagreements with some of those who had gone before you are aware of, and were present at, and I have heard you talk about them and [also his disagreements with] the views of some of the best intellects among the people of Medina [such as] Yaḥyā ibn Saʿīd, ʿUbaydallāh ibn ʿUmar, Kathīr ibn Farqad, and many others who were older than him, to the extent that what you didn't like about that forced you to leave his circle. I spoke with both you and ʿAbd al-ʿAzīz ibn ʿAbdallāh [ibn al-Mājishūn] with regard to some of what we consider unacceptable from Rabīʿa, and you were both in agreement about what I disagreed with, disliking the same things [from him] that I disliked. And yet, despite all this, by the grace of Allah, there was a lot of good in Rabīʿa: [he had] a sharp intellect, excellent Arabic, clear qualities, excellent behaviour in the *dīn*, and a love for his brothers generally and for us in particular. May Allah have mercy on him and forgive him, and reward him for the best of his actions.

There were also a lot of different opinions expressed by Ibn Shihāb, [both] when we met him and if any of us wrote to him, and sometimes he would write to someone about a matter, despite his extensive knowledge, with three different answers, each of which would contradict the other, without him realising what it was that he had said earlier about the matter. It is this that has caused me to discard those opinions that you did not want me to discard.[30]

Joining the prayers because of rain

Al-Layth then mentions a number of issues on which there was significant difference of opinion, sometimes even among the scholars of Medina. The first of them is that of joining between the prayers of *maghrib* and *ʿishāʾ* on rainy nights. Al-Layth says,

> You also know about my disliking his opinion that any one of the armies of the Muslims can join between [*maghrib* and *ʿishāʾ*] on a night when it is raining, although the rain in Syria is much more frequent than it ever is in Medina. No imam among them ever joined between prayers on a night when it was raining, although there were among them Abū ʿUbayda ibn al-Jarrāḥ, Khālid ibn al-Walīd, Yazīd ibn Abī Sufyān, ʿAmr ibn al-ʿĀṣ, Muʿādh ibn Jabal – and we have heard that the Messenger of Allah, may Allah bless him and grant him peace, said that Muʿādh was the most knowledgeable of them with regard to what is *ḥalāl* and what is *ḥarām*, and he also said that Muʿādh would come on the Day of Rising ahead of the men of knowledge by a long way – and Shurāḥibīl ibn Ḥasana, Abū l-Dardāʾ and Bilāl ibn Rabāḥ; and in Egypt there were Abū Dharr, al-Zubayr ibn al-ʿAwwām, and Saʿd ibn Abī Waqqāṣ; in Ḥimṣ there were seventy of those who had been at [the Battle of] Badr and in the Muslim armies as a whole; and in Iraq there were Ibn Masʿūd, Ḥudhayfa ibn al-Yamān, ʿImrān ibn Ḥuṣayn, and the Commander of the Faithful ʿAlī ibn Abī Ṭālib – may Allah ennoble his face for long years in the Garden – and there were [other] Companions of the Messenger of Allah, may Allah bless him and grant him peace, with him, and none of them ever joined between *maghrib* and *ʿishāʾ*.[31]

The issue of joining between *maghrib* and *ʿishāʾ* because of rain was indeed an issue on which there was difference of opinion between scholars, but Mālik, in the *Muwaṭṭaʾ*, is clear that, in his opinion, this is acceptable. In the section on 'Joining between two prayers when resident and when travelling',[32] Mālik mentions a report from Ibn ʿAbbās that the Prophet prayed *ẓuhr* and *ʿaṣr* together, and also *maghrib* and *ʿishāʾ* together, when it was neither a situation of fear nor of being on a journey, to which Mālik then adds, 'I think that was because of rain.' He then immediately follows this with a report from ʿAbdallāh ibn ʿUmar to the effect that, if the *amīr*s joined between *maghrib* and *'isha'* because of rain, he would join with them.[33] Al-Shaybānī doesn't mention the report from Ibn ʿAbbās and Mālik's comment after it, but he does mention the report about ʿAbdallāh ibn ʿUmar joining the prayers if the *amīrs* did so, although he then says, 'We don't go by this. We don't join between two prayers at one time, except for *ẓuhr* and *ʿaṣr* at 'Arafa, and *maghrib* and *ʿishāʾ* at Muzdalifa.' He then adds, 'We have heard that ʿUmar ibn al-Khaṭṭāb wrote to people in the provinces forbidding them from joining between two prayers, and informing them that joining between two prayers at [any] one time is a major wrong action.'[34] Indeed, it was Abū Ḥanīfa's view, like that of al-Layth ibn Saʿd, that the prayers should never be joined because of rain. But Mālik's view was that of his teacher Hishām ibn ʿUrwa, who said that he saw Abān ibn ʿUthmān joining the prayers because of rain, and with him were ʿUrwa ibn al-Zubayr, Saʿīd ibn al-Musayyab, Abū Salama ibn ʿAbd al-Rahmān and Abū Bakr ibn ʿAbd al-Rahmān, and none of them expressed any objection to him doing that. Similarly, ʿUbaydallāh ibn ʿUmar said that he saw Sālim and al-Qāsim doing the prayer (with the implication of them joining the prayers) with the *amīrs* on rainy nights. This was also the view of Aḥmad ibn Ḥanbal, while al-Shāfiʿī held the view that one could join not just between *maghrib* and *ʿishāʾ* but also between *ẓuhr* and *ʿaṣr*, if the rain was persistent.[35] So, although it may have been the case that the people in Syria were not of the habit of joining the prayers on nights when it was raining, the same cannot be said about the people of Medina, for whom it was clearly a well-known practice. Perhaps, contrary to what al-Layth suggests, it was precisely because heavy rain was so much less frequent in Medina than in Syria that the judgement of joining the prayers was allowed in Medina, since the occurrence of rain there was a lot more exceptional and so permitted this exception to the general rule.

Making a judgement with only one witness and the oath of the plaintiff

The second example al-Layth mentions is that of arriving at a judgement on the basis of the testimony of only one witness along with the oath of the plaintiff (as opposed to that of two male witnesses, or that of one man and two women). He says,

> You know that this is still used as a basis for judgement in Medina, although the Companions of the Messenger of Allah, may Allah bless him and grant

> him peace, did not judge by it, whether in Damascus or Hims or Egypt or Iraq, nor did the Rightly Guided Caliphs Abū Bakr, ʿUmar, ʿUthmān and ʿAlī write to them about it. Then ʿUmar ibn ʿAbd al-ʿAzīz became caliph, and he, as you know, was full of concern about bringing *sunna*s to life, along with his seriousness in putting the *dīn* into practice, and his hitting the mark with regard to his opinions, and his knowledge of what people had done in the past. Ruzayq ibn Ḥakīm wrote to him saying, 'You used to judge on the basis of one witness and the oath of the plaintiff', and ʿUmar ibn ʿAbd al-ʿAzīz wrote back to him saying, 'We used to judge by that in Medina but we found the people of Syria not doing that and so we only judge on the basis of the testimony of two just men, or one man and two women.'[36]

Al-Layth's position is thus clear: although the people in Medina continue to judge according to this principle, it effectively goes against the rest of the Muslim community and should be rejected on that basis. For Mālik, however, the matter is not as clear-cut as that. In the relevant section in the *Muwaṭṭaʾ*, 'Judging on the basis of an oath with a single witness', Mālik spells out his argument in the face of others' objections:

> There are people who say that an oath with a single witness is not valid, taking as their argument the words of Allah, the Blessed and Exalted – and His word is the truth – 'And have two of your menfolk bear witness, or, if there are not two men, then one man and two women, from among those whom you are satisfied with as witnesses' [Q. 2:282], and saying that if someone does produce [another] man or two women [as witnesses] he is entitled to nothing and cannot be allowed to take an oath along with only one witness.
>
> Part of the argument against such people is to ask them what they would say if someone were to claim some property from another man [i.e. without having any witnesses]? Would not the one against whom the claim is being made [either] swear that the claim is false, in which case the claim would be dropped, or refuse to do so, in which case the claimant would be asked to swear an oath that his claim is true, and thus establish his claim against the other man as valid? This is something about which there is no disagreement among anybody, anywhere. Why then do people accept this, and where in the Book of Allah does it occur? If people accept this, then let them accept an oath with one witness, even though it is not in the Book of Allah, the Mighty and Glorious, and that what has been established as *sunna* (*mā*

> *maḍā min al-sunna*) is enough. However, sometimes people like to know what the correct view is and where the proof lies, and in what we have said is a sufficient clarification of what is unclear in this matter, God willing.[37]

In other words, it is a false expectation to expect to find all judgements in the Qur'an. Rather, there is the lived context of the Book. As Mālik says, 'what has been established as *sunna* is enough', that *sunna* being the one that was established and maintained in Medina, and thus provides a model for others.

The *zakāt* of joint owners

A third example will further clarify al-Layth's position and the nature of his objections. Al-Layth says,

> Another example is that I have heard that you say, about two joint owners (*khalīṭayn*) of property (*māl*), that it is not obligatory for them to pay *zakāt* until each one possesses an amount on which *zakāt* is necessary. However, in the document of ʿUmar ibn al-Khaṭṭāb it says that they are both liable to *zakāt* and should pay according to what each one owes (*yatarāddāni bi-l-sawiyya*). That was acted upon during the governorate of ʿUmar ibn ʿAbd al-ʿAzīz before you, and that of others, and is what Yaḥyā ibn Saʿīd transmitted to us and he was not of any lesser quality than the best of the scholars in his time, may Allah have mercy on him, and forgive him, and make the Garden his abode.[38]

But this is to assume just one explanation of the concept of joint ownership in ʿUmar's document. Mālik records this document in the chapter in the *Muwaṭṭa'* on '*Zakāt* on livestock', which ends with the words 'What is separate should not be joined together, and what is together should not be separated, out of fear of *zakāt*'.[39] Mālik then explains what he understands by this phrase, in the chapter entitled 'The *Zakāt* of associates',[40] as follows:

> Mālik said, about two associates (*khalīṭayn*): 'If there is one herdsman, one male animal, and one pasture, and one watering-place, then the two are associates (*khalīṭān*), even if each one of them knows which animals are his and which are the other man's. If someone doesn't know which animals are his, he is not an associate (*khalīṭ*) but a co-owner (*sharīk*).'

Mālik said:'It is not obligatory for either associate to pay *zakāt* until he has an amount on which he has to pay *zakāt*. The explanation (*tafsīr*) of that is, that, if one of the associates has forty or more sheep and the other one has less than forty sheep, the one who has forty sheep has to pay one sheep while the one who has less than that doesn't have to pay anything. If both of them have the minimum amount on which *zakāt* is due, they are considered together for the purposes of *zakāt*, and both of them have to pay *zakāt* on the combined amount. If one of them has a thousand or less sheep, on which *zakāt* is due, and the other has forty or more sheep, then they are associates and each one pays his contribution according to the number of animals he has – on the one with a thousand, his portion, and on the one with forty, his portion.'

Mālik said:'Two associates with camels are like (*bi-manzilat*) two associates with sheep: they are considered together for *zakāt* if each one has an amount on which *zakāt* is due. This is because the Messenger of Allah, may Allah bless him and grant him peace, said, "There is no *zakāt* on less than five camels", and 'Umar ibn al-Khaṭṭāb said, "On free-ranging sheep, if they come to forty, there is one sheep [to pay]." '

Mālik said:'This is what I like best out of what I have heard about the matter.'

Mālik said:''Umar said: "What is separate should not be added together, and what is together should not be separated, out of fear of *zakāt*", and that refers to people who have livestock.'

Mālik said:'The explanation (*tafsīr*) of the phrase "what is separate should not be added together" is that there should be three people who each have forty sheep, on each one of whom *zakāt* is [thus] due. Then, when the *zakāt* collector comes to them, they add them together so that they only have to pay one sheep [because between 40 and 119 sheep, only one sheep is due]. They are forbidden to do this. The explanation of the phrase "what is together should not be separated" is that two owners each have 101 sheep, and so would owe three sheep on that amount [because on 201 to 300 sheep, three sheep are due]. Then, when the *zakāt* collector comes, they divide up their sheep so that each one only has to pay one sheep. This is forbidden. And so it is said, "What is separate should not be added together, and what is together should not be separated, out of fear of *zakat*." '

Mālik said:'This is what I have heard about this.'

So Mālik is clearly aware of other views and is not saying his view is the only view but, rather, that he has heard this view and it is the one he likes best out of what he has heard.

The oath of *īlā*ʾ (abstention from marital intercourse)

Another example al-Layth mentions is the one we have mentioned earlier about *īlā*ʾ (see Chapter 4), on which there was significant difference of opinion in Medina and yet which seems by Mālik's time to have been resolved to an agreed position (*al-amru ʿindanā*). As we have seen, the difference of opinion concerned whether divorce automatically ensued after the four-month waiting period was up, and whether the ensuing divorce should be considered revocable (*rajʿī*) or irrevocable (*bāʾin*).

Al-Layth is thus concerned about *ikhtilāf* – differences of opinion. If there are differences of opinion, and especially if this is the case even in Medina, then why should people be obliged to follow one view rather than another? And if the supposed Medinan view is actually different from the vast majority of the rest of the *umma*, why should one be obliged to follow it at all?

Mālik's response, of course, is the one that we have already heard. As a group experience, Medina remains different in quality from that of any other city, which cannot claim as a lived experience that which the Medinans can claim. And although, as we have seen, textual reports may suggest a clear picture with only one side to it, the lived experience of Medina produced genuine exceptions to genuine norms, but they were just that – exceptions to otherwise agreed norms.

* * *

Modern controversies

Although it is clear that there has been – and still remains – the phenomenon of *ikhtilāf*, it seems that one of the most frequent criticisms of Mālik and his *madhhab* among Muslims today is that it somehow ignores the perceived unity of the community around *ḥadīth* and fosters a culture of inconsistency with regard to texts and, at the same time, an acceptance of merely human decision when that of Allah and His Messenger is (a) available (i.e. through Qur'an and *ḥadīth*) and (b) is enough. But what the examples above show is that it is the exception that proves the rule. There is general acceptance, for example, that one shouldn't walk in front of someone who is doing the prayer, but what should a person do if the mosque is so crowded, with gaps opening up left, right and centre as people move forward to fill them up after the *iqāma* has been called, that one has no choice but to walk in front of others if one wants to fill up a gap? (This is, of course, exactly the situation today in both Mecca and Medina at any of the prayer times.)

Similarly, although there is general acceptance that there are four ongoing *madhhab*s which are all acceptable, it is also acceptable to try to understand how this situation came about. Was it not one initial event that resulted in what we see later? The position of Mālik is that Medina is our best record of that initial phenomenon and its continuation. But, goes the counterargument, the Companions spread out in the lands, taking their knowledge with them and establishing communities wherever they went. This of course is true, but Rabīʿa's counterargument is the key one here: 'one thousand from one thousand is preferred by me to one from one'. And 'one thousand from one thousand' cannot, in this context, mean one thousand people transmitting the same *ḥadīth* or *ḥadīth*s from one thousand others – which is extremely unlikely to have occurred in Rabīʿa's time, and certainly not in any formal way. It has to have meant one thousand people (at least) taking their *dīn* by living example from one thousand others (at least), which takes us back to *ʿamal* and its particular form of transmission by action. And it makes a priori sense that the place where this matter first started and was first put into practice has a claim – and potentially a better claim than any other place – to first consideration. Medina, after all, was the focal point in the past; could it not, should it not, also be the focal point going forward in the future?

Furthermore, as Qadi ʿIyāḍ points out in his *Madārik*, it is the duty of every *muqallid* ('follower' i.e. one not entitled to exercise *ijtihād*, or independent legal judgement) to choose the imam that he thinks is the most worthy of being followed. In fact, he says, this is precisely the *ijtihād* that the *muqallid* is entitled to exercise with regard to his *dīn*.[41] Therefore, the claim of the followers of Mālik that their imam is the closest to the truth is entirely to be expected. It is not a rejection of the other *madhhab*s but a reasoned and reasonable judgement about one particular option, based on an assessment of the available evidence.

It is also equally clear that Medina is not seen as a 'monolithic *fiqh* entity' – as it has been expressed[42] – but rather a dominant position among possibilities.

Nevertheless, it is clear that Mālik's choice of judgements among these possibilities was one that he felt had the strongest claim to the truth. As he said about the *zakāt* of joint owners of livestock, 'This is what I like best out of what I have heard about the matter.' We also quoted him earlier (see Chapter 3) as saying, in the context of the agreed opinion of Medina,

> Where I have heard nothing from them, I have used my own judgement (*ijtahadtu*) and considered the matter according to the way (*madhhab*) of those I have met, until I felt that I had arrived at the truth, or near to it, so that it would not be outside the way of the people of Medina and their opinions, even though I had not heard that particular [judgement] directly.

The instance of *sadl al-yadayn* discussed earlier (see Chapter 4) seems to cause particular concern among certain Muslims of a pro-*ḥadīth* frame of mind. The existence of some thirty *ḥadīth*s in the standard collections, which seem to indicate that *qabḍ* is desirable, if not obligatory, when doing the prayer, is seen as irrefutable evidence that this is indeed the correct judgement.[43] And yet the Mālikīs (and also the Shīʿa and the Ibāḍīs) maintain that *sadl* is the preferred position. Historically, *sadl* has been the position followed throughout North and West Africa in particular, where the *madhhab* of Mālik has held sway until this day. There is an interesting anecdote recorded by Ibn Baṭṭūṭa (707–779/1303–1377) in his *Riḥla*, where he notes the following:

> When we entered this city [i.e. Sinop, in northern Turkey], its people saw us doing the prayer with *sadl*. They are Ḥanafīs, and do not know the *madhhab* of Mālik, nor the [Mālikī] way of doing the prayer, in which the preferred position is to do the prayer with *sadl*. Some of them had seen Shīʿa groups in the Hijaz and Iraq doing the prayer that way, and so they suspected us of having that *madhhab*. They asked us about that and we told them that we followed the *madhhab* of Mālik. They weren't convinced, however, and their suspicions remained firmly in their hearts, until the Sultan's deputy sent us a rabbit and told one of his servants to stay with us to see what we would do with it. We slaughtered it, cooked it, and ate it. The servant went back and told him, at which point their suspicions were removed and they sent us gifts of welcome – because the Shīʿa do not eat rabbit.[44]

This clearly shows the normality of the practice in Ibn Baṭṭūṭa's time – and, one can presume, for a long time before that (from before the time of Imam

Mālik) and for a long time after that (up until very recently, when *sadl* began to suffer a decline even in predominantly Māliki contexts). Furthermore, al-Layth ibn Saʿd, despite his objections to following Medinan *ʿamal* when the Medinans were not agreed on a matter, preferred doing the prayer with *sadl*, as did a number of other early jurists (although there were also others who considered both *sadl* and *qabḍ* to be equally acceptable).[45] At the very least, the simplistic 'black-or-white' understanding of many present-day observers has to be seriously nuanced.

When we come to non-Muslim scholars we find, quite naturally, a different set of qualms. Most notably, there is a strong reluctance to accept any of the 'early' sources as genuinely early. They have, so the argument goes, mostly been recorded only in much later exempla: how, then, can we be sure that the 'original' wording hasn't changed over time and been subject to, in their view, standard textual corruption? Again, while this may possibly be true in certain cases, the *Muwaṭṭaʾ* provides an excellent counter-example. For, as we have seen earlier, in the *Muwaṭṭaʾ* we have a text which is remarkably solid in its essentials, that is, the texts that are recorded in it, and it has been transmitted almost word for word not only by numerous transmitters in many different parts of the Muslim world but also by friend and foe alike, that is to say, both those in agreement with, and those in disagreement with, its basic position. Thus we find great scholars such as Imam al-Shaybānī and Imam al-Shāfiʿī frequently referring to exactly the same texts as all the other transmitters of the *Muwaṭṭaʾ*, as we have seen in numerous examples above, but who have nevertheless objected to the way Mālik understands the broader implications of the texts. Therefore, it is not the texts themselves that are in question, but rather the interpretation of them and the context in which they are viewed and understood.

Amongst modern 'Euro-American' scholars of Islam, there seems to be a particular prejudice against accepting the authenticity of earlier texts which goes under the guise of 'historical research' or the historical-critical method. Two names in particular are associated with this view, and it has become more or less dogma in 'Western' Islamic Studies circles to accept the broad outlines – if not all the details – of this view. These two names are those of Goldziher and Schacht. (It is significant for our present enquiry that these two scholars, as noted in the Introduction, are the authors of the articles on 'Fiḳh' in the first and second editions, respectively, of the *Encyclopaedia of Islam*.)

It was Goldziher who, in his highly influential *Muhammedanische Studien* (1889–90), was effectively the first Western scholar to suggest the massive fabrication of *ḥadīth* for religious, historical and social reasons. He concluded,

> We ... will probably consider by far the greater part of it [= the *ḥadīth* literature] as the result of the religious, historical and social development of Islam during the first two centuries.
>
> The *ḥadīth* will not serve as a document for the history of the infancy of Islam, but as a reflection of the tendencies which appeared in the community during the mature stages of its development.'[46]

Schacht, writing some sixty years later in his equally influential *The Origins of Muhammadan Jurisprudence* (1950), accepted and built upon what he called 'this brilliant discovery' of Goldziher's, claiming that his book

> will be found to confirm Goldziher's results and go beyond them in the following respects: a great many traditions [i.e. *ḥadīths*] in the classical and other collections were put into circulation only after Shāfiʿī's time; the first considerable body of legal traditions from the Prophet originated towards the middle of the second century, in opposition to slightly earlier traditions from the Companions and other authorities, and to the 'living tradition' of the ancient schools of law; traditions from Companions and other authorities underwent the same process of growth, and are to be considered in the same light, as traditions from the Prophet; the study of *isnāds* often enables us to date traditions; the *isnāds* show a tendency to grow backwards and claim higher and higher authority until they arrive at the Prophet; the evidence of legal traditions carries us back to about the year 100 AH only; at that time Islamic legal thought started from late Umayyad administrative and popular practice, which is still reflected in a number of traditions.[47]

We can only say that our studies on Mālik and his *Muwaṭṭaʾ* indicate a very different picture. It is true that most transmissions of the *Muwaṭṭaʾ* were written down considerably after Mālik's death. We have seen that the standard formula introducing each section in the transmission of Yaḥyā ibn Yaḥyā al-Laythī, for instance, is, 'Yaḥyā told me', with the 'me' in this instance being understood to refer to Yaḥyā's son ʿUbaydallāh, who died in 278 AH

(= 891 AD).[48] At the same time, if we find that multiple witnesses from widely separated geographical areas all tell us exactly the same story, which they all attribute to Mālik, then it is a very far-fetched conclusion to say that this material doesn't come from Mālik. And, if it comes from Mālik, then it seems a small step to trust him when he specifies those teachers from whom he says he actually got his individual reports, unless we are to impute to him a massive amount of lying, which goes against the tenor of all the testimonials that are available to us from widely varying sources.

Basing himself on his reading of different transmissions of the *Muwaṭṭa'*, Goldziher gained an 'unfavourable impression of the reliability of Islamic tradition in the second century' and criticized Mālik for looseness in his methods of transmission.[49] However, Goldziher based his comments on the two transmissions available to him, that is, those of Yaḥyā and al-Shaybānī, which, as we have seen, do not form a representative pair. If he had had access to – or considered the possibility of having access to – those of Abū Muṣʿab al-Zuhrī, Ibn Bukayr, al-Qaʿnabī and Suwayd, for instance, he would doubtless have arrived at different conclusions. Furthermore, Goldziher's criticism is not as unbiased as it might at first seem to be. He says, for example, that Mālik 'cares little about the *rijāl* [i.e. his sources]' since he 'takes over and passes on unhesitatingly *ḥadīth*s told by the erotic singer ʿUrwa ibn Udhayna',[50] but this is a highly questionable judgement. First, to say that Mālik 'cares little about the *rijāl*' runs counter to everything we know about Mālik's strict standards of criticism of his authorities, and we must therefore doubt very much whether Mālik took over and passed on any *ḥadīth* 'unhesitatingly'. Second, he relates, as we have seen earlier (see Chapter 2), only one *ḥadīth* from ʿUrwa ibn Udhayna and not '*ḥadīth*s', and that *ḥadīth* (which appears in at least four transmissions of the *Muwaṭṭa'* and also in the *Mudawwana*)[51] is about a personal experience of Ibn Udhayna when he went on *ḥajj* with his grandmother. Third, to describe Ibn Udhayna somewhat dismissively as merely a 'singer' (whether 'erotic' or otherwise, allowing for the pre-modern meaning of the word 'erotic') is unnecessarily misleading. The passage in the *Kitāb al-Aghānī* to which Goldziher refers actually describes him as 'one of the most respected love-poets of Medina, counted as a jurist and a *muḥaddith*' and mentions also that his grandfather transmitted from ʿAlī,[52] to which al-Zurqānī adds that he was considered trustworthy and of good character.[53] It is hardly blameworthy therefore that Mālik should transmit one *ḥadīth* from a man who was clearly considered to be a respected member of the cultural community of his time.

Schacht followed the same general line as Goldziher in regard to the attribution of the *Muwaṭṭa'* to Mālik, saying that 'it is not Mālik who composed, in the modern sense of the word, his work, but [his] students who, each according to his own fashion, edited the "text" of their teacher'.[54] Elsewhere he also traces the differences between the transmissions to Mālik's students, claiming that 'in those days very little stress was laid on an accurate repetition of such texts and great liberty was taken by the transmitters'.[55] However, he also allows that Goldziher's implicit expectation of a 'fixed text'[56] is inappropriate in the context of an orally taught text, since 'Mālik did not always give exactly the same form to his orally-delivered teaching'.[57] Furthermore, although he states that 'the different *riwāyas* ... differ in places very much',[58] he also acknowledges that some of them, for example, those of Ibn Wahb and Ibn al-Qāsim, closely resemble the *Muwaṭṭa'* of Yaḥyā ibn Yaḥyā.[59] Thus, as with Goldziher, his observations that the differences between the transmissions are due to the transmitters bears some weight in the case of al-Shaybānī, and perhaps Suwayd, but would seem to apply far less to the transmissions of Abū Muṣʿab, Ibn Bukayr and al-Qaʿnabī, whose chapter headings and main text are all very close if not almost identical to Yaḥyā's.

This raises the broader issue of the nature of 'books' in the early Islamic period. It may be strictly true that, as Schacht puts it, 'the evidence of legal traditions carries us back to about the year 100 AH only', if by that is meant the existence of written texts, since that is when the enterprise of writing down the *ḥadīth* – again, according to the traditional sources – began. It is part of the traditional picture that Abū Bakr ibn Ḥazm and Ibn Shihāb were both instrumental in compiling *ḥadīth* at the request of the caliph ʿUmar ibn ʿAbd al-ʿAzīz (r. 99–101/717–20), who was concerned that knowledge of the *sunna* might be lost if it were not collected and recorded in writing.[60] After ʿUmar's death, and particularly in the time of Hishām (r. 105–25/724–43), this project was expanded by Ibn Shihāb, to the extent that it is Ibn Shihāb who is credited with being the first to make a comprehensive collection of *ḥadīth*. Despite this collection, however, Ibn Shihāb seems not to have organized this material into a book, which is what Mālik and his contemporaries began doing, resulting in collections such as the *Muwaṭṭaʾ*. This activity thus marks the transition from an initially oral method of transmission to one which becomes associated with writing and, by extension, the production of 'books' and all that that entails in terms of authorship and presentation. In Mālik's time it is still primarily individual pieces of material, that is, reports, that are being transmitted, rather than a fixed overall form, although an overall form is involved (e.g. there are 'books', such as the Book of *Zakāt*, which for the most part contains certain chapters in a certain order, which is usually followed by the Book of Fasting, which for the most part contains certain chapters in a certain order, and so on and so forth). Thus, with predominantly oral transmission and/or 'publication', the question of 'Who wrote the *Muwaṭṭaʾ*?', or 'Is Mālik the author of the *Muwaṭṭaʾ*?', is effectively meaningless and has to be thought of in different terms. Mālik's material is first published orally and then is noted down and subsequently organized (or reorganized) not by him but – as Schacht notes – by his students, and/or his students' students, with all the possible – but still limited – variation that that might involve. Thus, it is pointless to have doubts about the attribution, and therefore the authenticity, of a 'book' such as the *Muwaṭṭaʾ* simply because it has not actually been 'written', in the 'published work' sense, by the author to whom it is attributed: it may not be a 'book' in the strict single-author sense expected in later times, but neither is it someone else's work. Thus, 'Mālik's' *Muwaṭṭaʾ* may not have been given a definitive shape (or shapes, if we consider the different transmissions to represent different 'shapes') until many years after his death, but that does not mean that the book cannot be attributed to him. He is indeed the originator of the work, but it is a work that starts off in the form of private written notes and records intended for publication orally in lectures, and is only later disseminated as an actual 'book' in its more modern sense, with an identifiable beginning, middle and end.[61]

More problematic, perhaps, is when there are seemingly different views recorded from the same individual – in a seemingly authentic manner – on the same subject (such as, for example, in the issue of *sadl al-yadayn* discussed above). But, while this is seen by many non-Muslim scholars to cast major doubts on the whole corpus of *ḥadīth* and its attribution to its supposed sources, this is not the only way to understand this phenomenon. First, an authority may indeed hold, or have held, differing views on a subject. Second, problems with the authenticity and accuracy of *ḥadīth* were well known to the early scholars of Islam, including Mālik. Mālik, for instance, comparing the situation between Medina and Iraq, referred to Iraq as 'the minting-house' of *ḥadīth*[62] and quoted the statement of Ibn Shihāb that '*ḥadīth*s leave us a handspan [in size] and come back to us as a cubit' – meaning, from Iraq.[63] This was one of the reasons why Mālik preferred *ʿamal* to *ḥadīth*, which, as we have seen, he considered to be 'more accurate than *ḥadīth*'. The third-century Iraqi scholar, Ibn Qutayba (d. 276/889), put the same idea in a more formal way:

> In our opinion, the truth is more likely to be established by consensus (*ijmāʿ*) than by the transmission of *ḥadīth* (*al-riwāya*). *Ḥadīth* may be subject to forgetfulness, error, uncertainties, different possible interpretations, and abrogation; someone trustworthy may transmit from someone who is not; there may be two different commands, both of which are possible, such as making either one or two *taslīm*s [at the end of the prayer]. Similarly, a man may have been present when the Prophet, may Allah bless him and grant him peace, gave a certain command and then been absent when he told [people] to do something different: he will then transmit the first command and not the second, because he does not know it. Consensus [i.e. in this context, the consensus of the people of Medina], however, is free from such vicissitudes. This is why Mālik, may Allah have mercy on him, sometimes transmits a *ḥadīth* from the Messenger of Allah, may Allah bless him and grant him peace, but then says, 'The *ʿamal* in our city is such-and-such', mentioning something that is different to the *ḥadīth*. [This is] because his city was the city of the Prophet, may Allah bless him and grant him peace, and if the *ʿamal* in his time had included such-and-such a practice, that would have become the *ʿamal* of the following generation, and the generation after them, and the generation after them – and it is not possible that all the people would have stopped doing something that they were all doing in his city at his time and then done something else instead – and one generation from one generation is a much greater number than one from one. Indeed, people have related many *ḥadīth*s with complete chains of authority and then not acted according to them.[64]

Thus, we are left with Ibn Qutayba's conclusion that 'the truth is more likely to be established by consensus' – meaning, in this context, the agreed position in Medina – than by the transmission of *ḥadīth*.

One final example will illustrate not only this key distinction between *ʿamal* and *ḥadīth* but also how an understanding of this point opens up an understanding of not only the standard Muslim position but also the standard non-Muslim position. In the *Muwaṭṭaʾ*, Mālik includes the following *ḥadīth* in the section entitled 'When allowing a wife the choice of staying married does not constitute a divorce':

> [Yaḥyā] told me, from Mālik, from ʿAbd al-Raḥmān ibn al-Qāsim, from his father, that ʿĀʾisha, the wife of the Prophet, may Allah bless him and grant him peace, married Ḥafṣa, the daughter of ʿAbd al-Raḥmān, to al-Mundhir ibn al-Zubayr while ʿAbd al-Raḥmān was away in Syria. When ʿAbd al-Raḥmān returned, he said, 'Should someone like me have this done to him? Should someone like me have decisions made about him without his consent?' So ʿĀʾisha spoke to al-Mundhir ibn al-Zubayr, and al-Mundhir said, 'It's in the hands of ʿAbd al-Raḥmān.' ʿAbd al-Raḥmān said, 'I would not go against a decision that you [ʿĀʾisha] have made', and so Ḥafṣa stayed with al-Mundhir, and there was no divorce.[65] [ʿAbd al-Raḥmān was ʿĀʾisha's brother, so his daughter Hafsa was ʿĀʾisha's niece; al-Mundhir's mother was Asmāʾ, ʿĀʾisha's sister, so al-Mundhir was ʿĀʾisha's nephew.]

In the *Mudawwana*, in the chapter on 'Marriage without a legal guardian', we find the following interchange between Saḥnūn and Ibn al-Qāsim:

> I [= Saḥnūn] said: 'In the *ḥadīth* of ʿĀʾisha, when she married Ḥafṣa, the daughter of ʿAbd al-Raḥmān, to al-Mundhir ibn al-Zubayr, was it not ʿĀʾisha who concluded the marriage contract?'

He [Ibn al-Qāsim] said: 'We do not know what the explanation (*tafsīr*) of this is, except that we assume that she appointed someone else to actually contract the marriage.'

I said: 'Would it not be the case, if she had appointed someone else, that the marriage would be invalid, according to Mālik, even if the girl's father gave his permission?'

He said: 'This *ḥadīth* has come down to us. If it had been accompanied by continuous *ʿamal* up until the time of those we met and from whom we took [knowledge], and they likewise from those *they* had met, it would be correct to follow it. But in fact it is like other *ḥadīth*s which are not accompanied by *ʿamal*, such as what has been related from the Prophet, may Allah bless

> him and grant him peace, regarding using perfume while in *iḥrām* [for *ḥajj* or *ʿumra*], and the report that has come down from him where he said, "A fornicator is no longer a believer when he fornicates, nor [is a thief] a believer when he steals", whereas Allah has revealed the punishment [for fornication] and [the punishment of] cutting off the hand [for stealing] only for believers. Various things have been related from the Companions which have not been bolstered [by anything else] or been considered strong enough [to be put into practice], while other things have been put into practice and been followed by most people and most of the Companions.
>
> 'This *ḥadīth* thus remains neither rejected as inauthentic nor acted upon. Rather, other *ḥadīth*s that were accompanied by practice have been acted upon and transmitted by the Successors of the Companions of the Prophet, may Allah bless him and grant him peace, from the Companions, and have then been transmitted from these Successors in the same way, without them either rejecting them as inauthentic or denying what has been transmitted. What was not acted upon is left aside without rejecting it as inauthentic, and what was acted upon is acted upon and accepted as authentic.
>
> '[In this case] the *ʿamal* which is well attested to and is accompanied by people's practice (*al-aʿmāl*) is [the judgement indicated by] the statement of the Prophet, may Allah bless him and grant him peace, "A woman should not be married without a legal guardian", and the statement of ʿUmar, "A woman should not be married without a legal guardian", and the fact that ʿUmar separated a man and a woman who had married without a legal guardian.'[66]

Schacht takes this passage as clearly stating that 'the "practice" appeared first and traditions from the Prophet and from Companions appeared later'.[67] What this particular passage in fact shows is not a contrast between *ḥadīth*s on the one hand and practice, unconnected to *ḥadīth*s, on the other, but rather a contrast between two types of *ḥadīth*, namely, those that were accompanied by *ʿamal* and those that were not. Furthermore, this particular *ḥadīth*, as is shown by its inclusion in the relevant section in at least three transmissions of the *Muwaṭṭaʾ*, as well as in the *Mudawwana*, is accepted as a trustworthy source with regard to one particular aspect of the law, namely, that if a woman is given the choice of staying with her husband or leaving him, and she chooses to remain with him, that does not constitute a divorce. The question about ʿĀʾisha acting as legal guardian although the girl's father – her normal legal guardian – was in principle available, is a secondary issue, and ʿĀʾisha's action is considered a special exception (*khuṣūṣiyya*) because of her particular status with regard to the Prophet.[68] It was an exception, and the exception proves the general rule that, as stated in the *ḥadīth* cited from ʿUmar in the second chapter of the Book of Marriage in the *Muwaṭṭaʾ*, no woman can get married without the consent of her guardian, or someone of her family with sound judgement, or the Sultan.[69]

Thus, it is that, when it comes to *ḥadīth*, it would be hard to find a more reliable access point than the *ḥadīth* transmitted by Mālik in his *Muwaṭṭaʾ*. Likewise, when it comes to the *ʿamal* of the people of Medina, it would be hard to find a more reliable access point than the knowledge of it transmitted by Mālik in his *Muwaṭṭaʾ*.

We are thus left with a picture of the *dīn* of Islam that is quite overtly based on more than just texts, however authoritative those texts may be. That is, even if we accept Qur'an and (authentic) *ḥadīth* as an agreed starting point for the later expansion of Islamic law in all its ramifications of theory (*uṣūl*) and detail (*furūʿ*), it must always be remembered that this *dīn* is primarily a *dīn* of action – 'Act, and Allah will see your actions, and His Messenger and the believers' (Q.9:105) – and that the strongest, and most effective, method of transmission is that of action, hence the authority of *ʿamal* that is continually referred to in the *Muwaṭṭaʾ*, all of which serves to remind us, as Rabīʿa and Ibn Qutabya both affirmed, that the real transmission of this business is not by the texts of the few, but by the actions of the many.

Conclusion

It will be clear from the above that in the *Muwaṭṭaʾ* we have a very strong textual tradition which fully confirms the traditional judgement of Mālik as a past master of *ḥadīth*. As Imam al-Shāfiʿī put it, 'If it's authentic *ḥadīth* you want, then it's Mālik you need.'[1] Mālik was also the one, as we have seen, on whom al-Bukhārī and Muslim and all the later compilers of *ḥadīth* built their work, and thus is at the basis of the whole written tradition of *ḥadīth* in Islamic scholarship and culture.

With regard to *ḥadīth*, one notes that, on the Muslim side, there has been, and continues to be, an extreme reluctance to accept the authority of *ʿamal* as a source of judgements, if there is even an awareness of the possibility; rather, texts are seen as paramount. But, as we have seen, for Mālik, *ʿamal* is effectively stronger than *ḥadīth* and is based on an understanding of the *dīn* having been transmitted primarily by the actions of people rather than texts, however authentic those texts may be.

On the non-Muslim side, there is a similar reluctance to recognize the authority of *ʿamal* both as a source of, and an extension to, the *sunna* of the Prophet; there is also a similar bias towards texts, although in this case a negative one, since if a text cannot be authoritatively dated to, for example, the time of the Prophet, it has to be assumed in their view that it does not go back to that time, and no individuals, it seems, are trustworthy enough to gainsay that assumption. We can only reiterate Mālik's argument about the Medinan way of calling the *adhān*, which, he says, has been called five times a day, every day, from the time of the Prophet until his time, in a known and trusted manner. (In tandem with this judgement, the received knowledge of the people of Medina from the earliest times onwards 'until today' is that there is no *adhān* or *iqāma* for the two Eid prayers, and this, Mālik says, is 'the *sunna* about which there is no dispute among us'.)[2] But if one does accept ʿ*amal* as an authoritative vehicle of transmission, a new understanding of *sunna* is opened up which is not equated with the texts of *ḥadīth* and therefore not liable to the same doubts and criticism.

In particular, it seems that one has to reconsider the phenomenon of *ikhtilāf*, or differences of opinion, as being a natural manifestation of the original message and not a door for criticism of it. As Ibn Mujāhid said, by way of preface to his book on the Seven Readers (and therefore Seven Readings) of the Qur'an that he wished to highlight in his time, 'People have differed with regard to readings as they have differed with regard to legal judgements.'[3] Thus, although the source is one – the message of the Prophet in both its Qur'anic and its *sunna*ic forms – there is room for difference in detail, and this is as true for the Qur'an as it is for the *sunna*, or perhaps we should say that it is as true for the *sunna* as it is for the Qur'an. Nevertheless, the message remains one: there is one Qur'an, one Prophet, one message and one encouragement to action.

Finally, we should not forget the comment recorded from Mālik, that 'knowledge is not a matter of knowing a lot of texts; knowledge is a light that Allah puts in the heart'.[4] We have also seen that for Mālik knowledge is meaningless unless it is accompanied by action, and thus his emphasis on ʿ*amal*. And if, as we have suggested above, he is the key access point for *ḥadīth*, it is even more so that he is the key access point for ʿ*amal*, which is itself a reminder that the *dīn* is lived and transmitted by action, not by texts. We end our enquiry, as we started it, with the reminder that al-Qāsim ibn Muḥammad said, 'I remember a time when people were not impressed by words,' by which, Mālik says, he was referring to action (ʿ*amal*): 'It is people's actions that are looked at, not their words.'[5]

Glossary

adhān	the call to prayer
ʿamal	action, practice, especially that based on the established legal principles and precepts of the Medinan community
amīr	governor, ruler; prince
ʿaqīqa	sacrifice of a sheep for a newborn child
dīn	'religion', but with the broader sense of 'life-transaction'
duʿāʾ	prayer, in the sense of supplication
fatwā	legal ruling
fiḳh	= *fiqh* (q.v.)
fiqh	lit. 'understanding', that is, of how to derive and apply the law from a knowledge of its sources; jurisprudence; collectively, the judgements of Islamic law
ḥadīth	textual report (or reports, when used collectively), especially of the Prophet and/or his Companions
ḥajj	pilgrimage (to Mecca, performed at a specific time of the year); the fifth of the Five Pillars of Islam
ḥalāl	lawful, allowed, permitted
ḥarām	unlawful, prohibited, forbidden
iḥrām	the special state involving certain restrictions of clothing and general behaviour that a person must be in when doing *ḥajj* (q.v.) or *ʿumra* (q.v.)
ijmāʿ	consensus
ijtihād	independent reasoning, especially as used to arrive at new judgements in the absence of any clear precedent
ikhtilāf	difference of opinion
īlāʾ	oath of abstinence from marital intercourse
imam	one who goes in front, one who leads the way; prayer leader; political leader; expert
iqāma	the shorter version of the *adhān* (q.v.) said immediately before the prayer is begun

ʿishāʾ	the late evening prayer
isnād	chain of authority, especially of a *ḥadīth* (q.v.)
iʿtikāf	retreat in a mosque for a period of days, especially in the last few days of Ramadan
jihād	struggle, especially fighting for the sake of Allah to establish Islam
jizya	'poll-tax'; a protection tax levied on adult males of non-Muslim communities living under Muslim rule
madhhab	school of law or jurisprudence
maghrib	the sunset prayer
mawlā	freed slave; also, patron (of a freed slave)
mawālī	pl. of *mawlā* (q.v.)
mudd	a measure, roughly equivalent to a double-handful of grain
muḥaddith	scholar or transmitter of *ḥadīth* (q.v.)
Muḥarram	the first month of the Muslim year
mukātab	slave who has made an arrangement to achieve his freedom after earning a certain amount of money, usually paid by instalments
musnad	(of a *ḥadīth*) provided with a complete *isnād* (q.v.)
qabḍ	doing the prayer with the right hand clasping the left arm at the wrist
qirāḍ	a type of commenda partnership between two parties, one of which provides the finance and the other the labour, with the profits being divided in an agreed manner
Ramadan	the ninth month of the Muslim year; the month of fasting, the fourth of the Five Pillars of Islam
raṭl	a weight (variously defined; the Baghdadi *raṭl* is roughly equivalent to 400 g)
riwāya	transmission
ṣāʿ	a measure consisting of four *mudd*s (q.v.)
sadl	doing the prayer with one's arms hanging by one's sides (as opposed to *qabḍ*) (q.v.)
sharḥ	(book of) commentary, especially of *ḥadīth* (q.v.)
Sharīʿa	the divinely revealed law (lit. 'pathway') of the Muslims
shaykh	teacher

sunna	normative practice or custom, especially of the Prophet
sultan	governor, ruler
tafsīr	lit. 'explanation'; (book of) commentary, particularly of the Qur'an
taslīm	saying '*al-salāmu ʿalaykum*' ('Peace be upon you') at the end of the prayer
ʿumra	the 'lesser' pilgrimage to Mecca, undertaken at any time of the year
wuḍūʾ	the 'minor' ablution, or act of purification, necessary after urination, defecation, sleeping, etc., before doing the prayer
zakāt	obligatory alms-tax; the third of the Five Pillars of Islam

Notes

Introduction

1 David Powers, *Studies in Qur'an and Ḥadīth: The Formation of the Islamic Law of Inheritance* (Berkeley: University of California Press, 1986), p. 1.

2 Norman Calder, *Studies in Early Muslim Jurisprudence* (Oxford: Clarendon Press, 1993), p. 19.

3 Christopher Melchert, *The Formation of the Sunni Schools of Law, 9th-10th Centuries C.E.* (Leiden: Brill, 1997), p. xxi.

4 See e.g. Herbert Berg, *The Development of Exegesis in Early Islam: The Debate over the Authenticiy of Muslim Literature from the Formative Period* (Richmond: Curzon Press, 2000); also Herbert Berg, ed., *Method and Theory in the Study of Islamic Origins* (Leiden: Brill, 2003).

5 Mariam Sheibani, Amir Toft and Ahmed El Shamsy, 'The Classical Period: Scripture, Origins, and Early Development', Chapter 16, in *The Oxford Handbook of Islamic Law*, ed. Anver M. Emon and Rumee Ahmed (Oxford: Oxford University Press, 2018).

6 See Alan Jones, 'The Dotting of a Script and the Dating of an Era: The Strange Neglect of PERF 558', *Islamic Culture*, 52 (1998), pp. 95–101.

7 See Ilkka Lindstedt, 'Writing, Reading, and Hearing in Early Muslim-era Arabic Graffiti', *International Qur'anic Studies Association* (2017). Available online: iqsaweb.wordpress.com/tag/ilka-lindstedt (accessed 23 February 2021). See now also al-Saʿīd et al., *Nuqūsh Ḥismā: kitābāt min ṣadr al-Islām shamāl gharb al-Mamlaka* (Riyadh: al-Majalla al-ʿArabiyya, 2017).

8 Hallaq, for instance, makes the pertinent comment that the *Muwaṭṭaʾ* 'is permeated by the notion of agreement, not disagreement' (Wael B. Hallaq, 'From Regional to Personal Schools of Law? A Reevaluation', *Islamic Law and Society*, 8 (2001), pp. 1–26, 11).

9 Thus, for example, Ahmed El Shamsy (*The Canonization of Islamic Law* (Cambridge: Cambridge University Press, 2013), p. 41) refers to 'the alliance formed by scholars and government officials' that put a stop to usurious speculation on shares in an expected food shipment at the market of al-Jār (see also p. xiv).

10 Mālik ibn Anas, *Al-Muwaṭṭa', The Royal Moroccan Edition, The Recension of Yaḥyā ibn Yaḥyā al-Laythī*, ed. Mohammed Fadel and Connell Monette (Cambridge, MA: Harvard University Press, 2019).

11 See Chapter 3. Also Hallaq, 'From Regional to Personal Schools?', p. 12 (citing the same passage, from Ibn Farḥūn's *al-Dībāj al-Mudhhab*).

12 See *Muw.* 1:201.

13 For this interplay between scholars and political authorities, see e.g. Yasin Dutton, *The Origins of Islamic Law: The Qur'an, the* Muwaṭṭa' *and Medinan* 'Amal (Richmond: Curzon, 1999), pp. 130–2, 219 n. 75; also ibid, 'Juridical Practice and Madinan *'Amal: Qaḍā'* in the *Muwaṭṭa'* of Mālik', *Journal of Islamic Studies*, 10, no. 1 (1999), pp. 1–21.

14 See *Muw.* 2:63. This particular incident is highlighted by El Shamsy, as noted above, n. 9.

15 See *Muw.* 2:63–4, 67–8.

16 See e.g. Umar Abd-Allah Wymann-Landgraf, *Malik and Medina: Islamic Legal Reasoning in the Formative Period* (Leiden: Brill, 2013), pp. 54–7, which mentions Melchert's defence of Calder's position but also Miklos Muranyi's strong rebuttal of the same; also Jonathan Brockopp, 'Competing Theories of Authority in Early Mālikī Texts', in *Studies in Islamic Legal Theory*, ed. Bernard G. Weiss (Leiden: Brill, 2002), pp. 4–5.

17 As cited in Brockopp, 'Competing Theories', pp. 17–18.

18 Ibid., p. 18.

19 *Muw.* 2:89.

20 *Muw.* 2:85.

21 *Muw.* 2:75.

22 See *Muw.* 2:54; also 2:68, 76.

23 *Muw.* 2:76–7.

24 *Muw.* 2:255; *Muw. al-Zuhrī*, 2:171; *Muw. Suwayd*, p. 599.

1 The man and his family

1 Aḥmad ibn Ḥanbal, *al-Musnad* (Beirut: Dār al-Fikr, 1414/1994), 3:160; al-Tirmidhī, *Sunan* [= *al-Jāmi' al-ṣaḥīḥ*] (Cairo: Maṭba'at Muṣṭafā al-Bābī al-Ḥalabī wa-Awlāduh, 1st edn, 1356/1937, 2nd edn, 1395/1975), 5:47–8.

2 See *Mad.* 1:110; Dutton, *Origins*, p. 182 n. 1.

3 See *Mad.* 1:115; Dutton, *Origins*, p. 182 n. 1.

4 For references, see Dutton, *Origins*, p. 182 n. 5.

5 *Mad.* 1:107; also Dutton, *Origins*, p. 182 n. 8.

6 See Dutton, *Origins*, p. 182 n. 16.
7 *Mad.* 1:109.
8 Ibn Jubayr, *Riḥla* (Beirut: Dār Ṣādir/Dār Bayrūt, 1384/1964), pp. 173–4.
9 This identification of Nāfiʿ as the Medinan Qur'an reciter, rather than Nāfiʿ, the *mawlā* of Ibn ʿUmar (as is sometimes erroneously suggested), was confirmed to me personally in Medina by Mr ʿAbdallāh Kābir, researcher in the Centre for Research and Studies of al-Madina al-Munawwara (personal communication, April 2014).
10 See e.g. www.duas.org/baqi8shawwal.htm (accessed 23 February 2021).

2 His teachers

1 *Tam.* 6:108.
2 *Tam.* 6:112.
3 *Tam.* 6:107.
4 Ibid.
5 *Tam.* 6:109.
6 For references to ʿUmar's document, see *Muw.* 1:195–6, 198–9; for references to ʿAmr ibn Ḥazm's document, see *Muw.* 1:157, 2:181, 186.
7 *Muw. Sh.*, p. 330.
8 For a useful coverage of the question of Ibn Shihāb's relationship with the Umayyads, see Michael Lecker, 'Biographical Notes on Ibn Shihāb al-Zuhrī', *Journal of Semitic Studies*, 41 (1996), pp. 21–63, esp. pp. 22–41 [reprinted in Michael Lecker, *Jews and Arabs in Pre- and Early Islamic Arabia*, Section XVI (Aldershot: Ashgate Variorum, 1999)].
9 For the role of the political authorities in collecting *zakāt*, and the Qur'anic verses indicating this (particularly Q.9:60 and 103), see Yasin Dutton, 'The Qurʾān as a Source of Law: The Case of *Zakāt* (Alms-Tax)', in *Islamic Reflections Arabic Musings: Studies in Honour of Alan Jones*, ed. Robert G. Hoyland and Philip F. Kennedy (Oxford: Gibb Memorial Trust, 2004), pp. 201–16, esp. pp. 203–8.
10 *Tam.* 6:112; also Lecker, 'Biographical Notes', p. 37.
11 *Tam.* 7:58–9.
12 *Tam.* 8:5.
13 Ibn Saʿd, *al-Ṭabaqāt al-kubrā*, ed. ʿAlī Muḥammad ʿUmar (Cairo: Maktabat al-Khānjī, 1421/2001), 7:509.
14 *Tam.* 6:303.
15 *Tam.* 7:58.
16 *Tam.* 9:209.

17 *Tam.* 8:6; also 6:307.
18 *Tam.* 9:7.
19 *Tam.* 9:9.
20 *Tam.* 7:60.
21 *Tam.* 9:207, 209.
22 *Tam.* 7:58 n. 6.
23 *Tam.* 16:49.
24 *Tam.* 9:119; cf. *Tam.* 3:151.
25 *Tam.* 9:120.
26 Ibid.
27 *Tam.* 9:119–20.
28 *Tam.* 8:394.
29 *Isʿāf*, p. 24.
30 *Tam.* 7:60.
31 *Tam.* 13:239.
32 *Tam.* 13:237.
33 Wakīʿ, *Akhbār al-quḍāt*, ed. Saʿīd Muḥammad al-Laḥḥām (Beirut: ʿĀlam al-Kutub, n.d.), p. 119.
34 *Tam.* 23:89.
35 See *Tam.* 18:6–8.
36 *Tam.* 18:6.
37 *Tam.* 3:241.
38 *Tam.* 3:242.
39 Ibn Abī Ḥātim, *Kitāb al-Jarḥ wa-l-taʿdīl* (Hyderabad: Dāʾirat al-Maʿārif al-ʿUthmāniyya, 1360/1941), 1:21, 9:337.
40 *Tam.* 17:156.
41 *Tam.* 1:198.
42 *Tam.* 21:145; Zur. 1:76.
43 *Tam.* 21:146.
44 *Tam.* 22:7.
45 *Mad.* 1:119.
46 *Tam.* 3:2.
47 *Tam.* 21:236.
48 Ibn Farḥūn, *al-Dībāj al-mudhhab*, ed. Maʾmūn ibn Muḥyī al-Dīn al-Jannān (Beirut: Dār al-Kutub al-ʿIlmiyya, 1417/1996), p. 58.
49 *Tam.* 20:183.
50 *Tam.* 20:269; also *Muw.* 1:260.
51 *Tam.* 2:67.
52 See *Tam.* 2:67.
53 *Tam.* 12:222.

54 *Tam*. 17:416.
55 Wakīʿ, *Quḍāt*, p. 100.
56 For these and similar inscriptions, see Ali al-Ghabban, *Les deux routes syrienne et égyptienne de pèlerinage au nord-ouest de l'Arabie Saoudite* (Cairo: Institute français d'archéologie orientale, 2011), and Ḥayāt al-Kilābī, *al-Nuqūsh al-Islāmiyya fī ṭarīq al-ḥajj al-Shāmī shimāl gharb al-Mamlaka al-ʿArabiyya al-Saʿūdiyya, min al-qarn al-awwal ilā l-qarn al-khāmis al-Hijrī* (al-Riyadh: Maktabat al-Malik Fahd al-Waṭaniyya, 2009); also, for the second of these two inscriptions in particular, Frédéric Imbert, 'Califes, princes et compagnons dans les graffiti du debut de l'Islam', *Romano-Arabica*, 15 (2015), pp. 70, 78. I am grateful to Mr Ghali Adi for alerting me to these inscriptions and references. See also Introduction, n. 7.
57 *Tam*. 20: 5.
58 Wakīʿ, *Quḍāt*, 1:167.
59 *Muw*. 1:314; *Muw. Sh*., p. 262; *Muw. al-Zuhrī*, 2:208; *Muw. Suwayd*, p. 262; *Mud*. 2:82.
60 *Mad*. 1:120.
61 *Mad*. 1:120; Dutton, *Origins*, p. 12.
62 *Mud*. 1:135, 3:105, 4:135.
63 *Bayān*, 1:52, 7:212, 10:25, 17:41, 18:447.
64 *Tam*. 3:4; Dutton, *Origins*, p. 183 n. 20.

3 The *Muwaṭṭaʾ*

1 See Dutton, *Origins*, p. 187 nn. 1 and 2.
2 *Mad*. 1:83.
3 *Mad*. 1:133–4.
4 *Mad*. 1:133.
5 *Mad*. 1:132.
6 *Mad*. 1:191.
7 *Mad*. 1:196.
8 *Muw*., Introduction, 1:5.
9 *Muw. Sh*., Introduction, p. 13.
10 Shāh Walī Allāh al-Dihlawī, *Ḥujjat Allāh al-Bāligha*, ed. Muḥammad Sharīf Sukkar (Beirut: Dār Iḥyāʾ al-ʿUlūm, 1410/1990), 1:385–6.
11 See *Muw*. 1:232–6.
12 See Ibn Ḥajar al-ʿAsqalānī, *Tahdhīb al-tahdhīb* (Hyderabad: Dāʾirat al-Maʿārif al-Niẓāmiyya, 1325–7/1907–9), 11:301; also *Mad*. 2:537.

13 See Dutton, *Origins*, p. 16.
14 See *Muw.*, Introduction, pp. 7–8.
15 *Muw. al-Zuhrī*, Introduction, pp. 41–2.
16 See *Muw. al-Zuhrī*, Introduction, pp. 40–1.
17 See *Muw. Ibn Ziyād*, Introduction, p. 69.
18 A copy of this transmission is currently being prepared, from a number of copies of it, by Prof. Bashshār ʿAwwād Maʿrūf, as referred to in a lecture given by him at SOAS, London, 24 October 2019, entitled 'The Muwatta' of Malik ibn Anas: Variations among Its Recensions and Their Rationale'. Recording available at http://www.iccuk.org/news2.php?section=news&page=news195 (accessed 24 February 2021).
19 See Joseph Schacht, 'Deux éditions inconnues du *Muwaṭṭa'*', in *Studi Orientalistici in Onore di Giorgio Levi Della Vida*, vol. 2 (Rome: Istituto per l'Oriente, 1956); idem., 'On Some Manuscripts in the Libraries of Morocco', *Hespéris-Tamuda*, 9 (1968).
20 *Muw.*, Introduction, p. 7.
21 *Mad.* 1:398.
22 A complete copy of this transmission is referred to by Prof. Bashshār ʿAwwād Maʿrūf in the lecture he gave at SOAS, London, 24 October 2019 (see n. 18 above).
23 A manuscript in Istanbul containing significant portions of both the transmissions of Ibn al-Qāsim and Ibn Wahb is referred to by Prof. Bashshār in his lecture given at SOAS (see n. 18 above).
24 *Mad.* 1:436.
25 A manuscript in Istanbul containing significant portions of both the transmissions of Ibn al-Qāsim and Ibn Wahb is being prepared for publication by Prof. Bashshār (lecture given at SOAS; see n. 23 above.)
26 See also n. 25 above, for a manuscript containing portions of the transmission of Ibn Wahb along with that of Ibn al-Qāsim.
27 See Ibn Wahb, *al-Muwaṭṭa'*, ed. Hishām ibn Ismāʿīl al-Ṣīnī (Hofuf: Dār ibn al-Jawzī, 1420/1999).
28 See Zur. 1:8; Mohamed El Mokhtar Ould Bah, *Madkhal ilā uṣūl al-fiqh al-Mālikī* (Rabat: Dār al-Amān, 2011), p. 171; *Muw. Ibn Ziyād*, Introduction, p. 77.
29 See Ahmed El Shamsy, 'Al-Shāfiʿī's Recension of Mālik's *Muwaṭṭa'*', https://islamiclaw.blog/2019/12/06/muwaṭṭa'-roundtable-al-shafiʿis-recension-of-maliks-muwaṭṭa' (accessed 23 February 2021).
30 For these equivalences, see e.g. Yasin Dutton, 'Islam and the Environment: A Framework for Enquiry', in *Islam and the Environment*, ed. Harfiyyah Abdel Haleem (London: Ta-Ha, 1998), p. 61 and associated footnotes.
31 *Muw.* 1;188.

32 See *Muw. Zuh.*, 1:249–50.

33 Nadhīr Ḥamdān, *al-Muwaṭṭa'āt* (Damascus: Dār al-Qalam, 1412/1992), pp. 118–19.

34 *Muw. Suwayd*, pp. 222–3.

35 *Muw. Sh.*, pp. 114–15.

36 For this interpretation, see e.g. Zur. 2:44.

37 For this interpretation, see e.g. *Muw.* 1:189; Zur. 2:45; al-Baji, *al-Muntaqā, Sharḥ Muwaṭṭa' al-Imām Mālik*, 7 vols (Beirut: Dār al-Kitāb al-ʿArabī, n.d.) (originally Cairo: Maṭbaʿat al-Saʿāda, 1331–2/1913–14), 2:96.

38 *Muw.* 1:189–90.

39 See *Muw. Zuh.*, 1:251–4.

40 See Ḥamdān, *al-Muwaṭṭa'āt*, p. 119.

41 See *Muw. Suwayd*, p. 223.

42 See *Muw. Sh.*, p. 115.

43 See *Muw.* 1:209.

44 *Muw. al-Zuhrī*, 1:269.

45 *Muw. al-Zuhrī*, 1:380–1.

46 See *Muw. al-Zuhrī*, 1:291–2.

47 See *Muw.* 1:206–8.

48 *Muw. Sh.*, p. 117.

49 See *Muw. al-Qaʿnabī*, pp. 198–204. (The report from ʿUrwa occurs on p. 202.)

50 See *Muw. Suwayd*, pp. 222–6.

51 See *Muw. Sh.*, pp. 114–20. (The exception is the 'Chapter on *kanz*' i.e. wealth on which *zakāt* has not been paid (p. 120), which contains no report from Abū Ḥanīfa.)

52 *Muw.* 1:212; *Muw. al-Zuhrī*, 1:301; *Muw. Sh.*., p. 130.

53 Ḥamdān, *al-Muwaṭṭa'āt*, p. 119; *Muw. Suwayd.* p. 413.

54 *Muw.* 1:211–28.

55 *Muw. al-Zuhrī*, 1:299–300.

56 *Muw.* 1:72–3.

57 *Muw.* 1:133.

58 *Muw. al-Zuhrī*, 1:78–9, 164.

59 Ḥamdān, *al-Muwaṭṭa'āt*, p. 117.

60 *Muw. al-Qaʿnabī*, pp. 204–7.

61 See *Muw. Suwayd*, pp. 411–14.

62 See *Muw. Sh.*, pp. 122, 128, 130.

63 *Muw. al-Zuhrī*, 1:301; Ḥamdān, *al-Muwaṭṭa'āt*, p. 117; *Muw. al-Qaʿnabī*, p. 207; *Muw. Suwayd*, p. 413.

64 See *Muw.* 1:211–27, 294.

65 See *Muw. al-Zuhrī*, 1:343–4, 527–9.

66 See *Muw. al-Qaʿnabī*, pp. 204–30.
67 See *Muw. Suwayd*, pp. 411–32.
68 See *Muw. Sh.*, pp. 122–31.
69 We note El Shamsy's comment that al-Shāfiʿī's transmission 'seems to be closer to [that] of Abū Muṣʿab than that of Yaḥyā', which accords with our general findings here with regard to Yaḥyā's transmission compared with the others available. See El Shamsy, 'Al-Shāfiʿī's Recension of Mālik's *Muwaṭṭa*'.
70 Sarah Savant has suggested that al-Shaybānī's transmission is more of a commentary than a transmission, but I would prefer to think of it as a re-presentation of very similar material with comments – rather than a commentary – relating to his understanding (*fiqh*) of the material, and hence his frequent reference to Abū Ḥanīfa's views and not to Mālik's. See Sarah Savant, 'A Tale of 3 "Versions"', *KITAB website*, September 10, 2017, http://kitab-project.org/2017/09/10/a-tale-of-3-versions/ (accessed 23 February 2021).
71 *Mad.* 1:194.

4 The ʿ*amal* of the people of Medina

1 *Muw.* 1:146; *Muw. al-Zuhrī*, 1:227; *Muw. Suwayd*, p. 201.
2 *Muw.* 1:328–9; *Muw. al-Zuhrī*, 2:206; *Muw. Suwayd*, pp. 384–5.
3 *Muw. Ibn Ziyad*, p. 136. Cf. *Muw. Sh.*, pp. 225–6, where, although the same *ḥadīth*s are mentioned, there is, characteristically, no mention of ʿ*amal*.
4 *Muw.* 1:111; *Muw. al-Zuhrī*, 1:122; *Muw. Suwayd*, p. 122.
5 *Muw.* 2:123–4; also *Muw. al-Zuhrī*, 2:470–1, and *Muw. Suwayd*, p. 279, where only the first part of this judgement is mentioned.
6 *Muw.* 1:205; *Muw. al-Zuhrī*, 1:285.
7 *Muw.* 2:70; *Muw. al-Zuhrī*, 2:359.
8 *Muw.* 2:77; *Muw. al-Zuhrī*, 2:376
9 Cf. Jonathan Brockopp, Review of Dutton, *Origins of Islamic Law*, in *Journal of Islamic Law and Society*, 7 (2000), pp. 398–400, for a rather different understanding of the matter.
10 *Mad.* 1:64–5.
11 Muḥammad al-Ṭālib Ibn Ḥamdūn, *Ḥāshiya ʿalā sharḥ Mayyāra al-ṣughrā li-manẓūmat al-Murshid al-muʿīn li-ʿAbd al-Wāḥid ibn ʿĀshir* (Beirut: Dār al-Fikr, 1392/1972), 1:16.
12 *Muw.* 2:208.
13 Although some doubt has been expressed by Hallaq and Lowry in particular about whether al-Shāfiʿī is actually the originator of a 'four-sources' theory

of law (see Wael B. Hallaq, 'Was al-Shāfiʿī the Master Architect of Islamic Jurisprudence?' *International Journal of Middle East Studies*, 25 (1993), pp. 587–605; idem., *The Origins and Evolution of Islamic Law* (Cambridge: Cambridge University Press, 2005), pp. 117–20, 128; Joseph Lowry, 'Does Shāfiʿī Have a Theory of "Four Sources" of Law?' in *Studies in Islamic Legal Theory*, ed. Bernard G. Weiss (Leiden: Brill, 2002), pp. 23–50), there is no denying that al-Shāfiʿī does mention all these four sources in his *Risāla* – as Lowry's citations and Hallaq's argument clearly demonstrate – and does seem to condemn any method beyond them (such as *istiḥsān*, or 'what someone deems good', for example) as being too far divorced from the revealed texts (*bayān*) that for him should form the sole basis of Islamic law. Thus, at the very least, al-Shāfiʿī can be credited, as Hallaq allows, with 'advocat[ing] the [four-sources] Synthesis in a rudimentary form' (Hallaq, *Origins*, p. 128).

14 *Mad.* 1:192.

15 *Mad.* 1:67–8.

16 *Mad.* 1:66. To the best of my knowledge, this important passage was highlighted for the first time in English by Shaykh Abdalqadir al-Murabit in his *Root Islamic Education*, pp. 72–3.

17 *Muw.* 2:18–19.

18 *Muw.* 1:260–1.

19 *Muw.* 1:133.

20 *Mud.* 1:74.

21 Muḥammad Ḥabīballāh Ibn Māyaʾbā al-Shinqīṭī, *Iḍāʾat al-ḥālik min alfāẓ dalīl al-sālik ilā Muwaṭṭaʾ al-Imām Mālik*, 2nd edn (Beirut: Dār al-Bashāʾir al-Islamiyya, 1415/1995), p. 82.

22 Ibid., p. 76.

23 Ibid., p. 78 n. 9.

24 Muḥammad Aḥmad ʿIllīsh, *Fatḥ al-ʿalī al-mālik fī l-fatwā ʿalā madhhab al-Imām Mālik* (Beirut: Dār al-Fikr, 1392/1972), 1:25.

25 *Mad.* 1:224–5.

5 Controversies, ancient and modern

1 *Muw.* 1:130–2.

2 *Muw. al-Zuhrī*, 1:159–62, esp. p. 162.

3 *Muw. Sh.*, pp. 97–98.

4 Muḥammad ibn al-Ḥasan al-Shaybānī, *Kitāb al-Ḥujja ʿalā Ahl al-Madīna*, ed. Mahdī Ḥasan al-Kīlānī al-Qādirī, 3rd edn (Beirut: ʿĀlam al-Kutub, 1403/1983), 1:218–22.
5 Ibid.
6 Ibid., 1:222.
7 *Muw.* 1:190–1.
8 For this interpretation, see Zur. 4:46–7.
9 *Muw.* 2:191, referring to *Muw.* 2:182.
10 *Muw. Sh.*, p. 119.
11 *Muw. Sh.*, pp. 232–3; for the last *ḥadīth*, see *Muw.* 2:123.
12 al-Shaybānī, *Kitāb al-Ḥujja*, 1:428–47.
13 *Muw.* 1:42–3.
14 *Muw.* 1:35–6.
15 *Muw. Sh.*, p. 54.
16 *Muw. Sh.*, pp. 42–3.
17 *Mud.* 1: 5–6.
18 Muḥammad ibn Idrīs al-Shāfiʿī, *Kitāb al-Umm* (in the section *Kitāb Ikhtilāf Mālik wa-l-Shāfiʿī*), (Beirut: Dār al-Fikr, 1400/1980), 7:221–2.
19 *Muw.* 2:121.
20 *Muw. Sh.*, p. 296.
21 *Mud.* 6:195.
22 See *Muw.* 2:122.
23 See ibid.
24 See *Muw.* 2:122–3 (with slight differences).
25 See *Muw.* 2:123.
26 al-Shāfiʿī, *Kitāb al-Umm* (in the section *Kitāb Ikhtilāf Mālik wa-l-Shāfiʿī*), 7:243–4.
27 *Mad.* 1:196.
28 Ibid.
29 See, for example, al-Dhahabī, *Tadhkirat al-Ḥuffāẓ* (Hyderabad: Dāʾirat al-Maʿārif al-ʿUthmaniyya, 1377/1958), 1:224; al-Abshīhī, *al-Mustaṭraf* (al-Manṣūra: Dār al-Ghad al-Jadīd, 1430/2009), p. 30.
30 al-Fasawī, *Kitāb al-Maʿrifa wa-l-Tārīkh* (al-Madīna al-Munawwara: Maktabat al-Dār, 1410/1990), 1:688–90.
31 Ibid., 1:690–1.
32 *Muw.* 1:122–4.
33 These two reports occur together, in the same order, in the transmissions of al-Zuhrī (*Muw. al-Zuhrī*, 1:144–5); al-Qaʿnabī (*Muw. al-Qaʿnabī*, pp. 185–6); and Suwayd (*Muw. Suwayd*, pp. 140–1).
34 *Muw. Sh.*, p. 82.

35 See *Tam.* 12:210–13.
36 al-Fasawī, pp. 691–2.
37 *Muw.* 2:110; *Muw. al-Zuhri*, 2:475–6.
38 al-Fasawī, 1:694.
39 *Muw.* 1:195–6; *Muw. al-Zuhri*, 1:264–6.
40 *Muw.* 1:198–9; *Muw. al-Zuhri*, 1:270–2; *Muw. al-Qa'nabi*, pp. 198–201
41 See *Mad.* 1:76.
42 See e.g. G. F. Haddad, Review of Dutton, *Original Islam: Mālik and the Madhhab of Madina*, *Muslim World Book Review*, 27, no. 4 (summer 2007), p. 34.
43 For these *ḥadīth*s, see Dutton, '*ʿAmal v. Ḥadīth* in Islamic Law: The Case of *Sadl al-yadayn* (Holding One's Hands by One's Sides) When Doing the Prayer', *Islamic Law and Society*, 3 (1996), esp. pp. 17–25.
44 Ibn Baṭṭūṭa, *Riḥla* (Beirut: Dār Ṣādir, n.d.), p. 302.
45 See *Tam.* 20:75.
46 Ignaz Goldziher, *Muslim Studies*, trans. C. R. Barber and S. M. Stern (London: George Allen & Unwin, 1967–71), 2:19.
47 Joseph Schacht, *The Origins of Muhammadan Jurisprudence* (Oxford: Clarendon Press, 1950), pp. 4–5.
48 See Zur. 1:12.
49 Goldziher, *Muslim Studies*, 2:204–5.
50 Ibid., 2:135.
51 See *Muw.* 1:314; *Muw. al-Zuhrī*, 2:208, *Muw. Suwayd*, p. 262, *Muw. Sh.*,p. 262; *Mud.* 2:82.
52 *al-Aghānī*, 18:330.
53 Zur. 2:333.
54 Schacht, 'Deux editions', p. 477.
55 Joseph Schacht, 'Mālik b. Anas', in *Encyclopaedia of Islam*, 2nd edn, vol. 6 (Leiden: E.J. Brill, 1991), p. 264.
56 See Goldziher, *Muslim Studies*, 2:205.
57 Schacht, "Mālik", p. 264.
58 Ibid.
59 Ibid.; idem., 'On Some Manuscripts in Kairouan and Tunis', *Arabica*, 14 (1967), p. 230.
60 See e.g. *Muw. Sh.*, p. 330.
61 For the general ideas in this paragraph, see particularly Gregor Schoeler, *The Genesis of Literature in Islam: From the Aural to the Read* (Edinburgh: Edinburgh University Press, 2009), a revised edition and translation (by Shawkat Toorawa) of the author's French book *Écrire et transmettre dans les débuts de l'Islam*.
62 See *Mad.* 1:234.

63 Ibn Saʿd, 7:435.

64 Ibn Qutayba, *Taʾwīl mukhtalif al-ḥadīth*, ed. Muḥammad Zuhrī al-Najjār (Beirut: Dār al-Jīl, 1393/1972), pp. 261–2.

65 *Muw.* 2:18; *Muw. Sh.*, pp. 191–2; *Muw. al-Zuhrī*, 1:603; *Muw. Suwayd*, p. 323.

66 *Mud.* 2:178.

67 Schacht, *Origins*, p. 63.

68 Zur. 3:38.

69 *Muw.* 2:3; *Muw. Sh.*, pp. 181–2; *Muw. al-Zuhrī*, 1:569–70.

Conclusion

1 *Mad.* 1:130.

2 See *Muw.* 1:146; *Muw. al-Zuhrī*, 1:227; *Muw. Suwayd*, p. 201.

3 Ibn Mujāhid, *Kitāb al-Sabʿa fī l-qirāʾāt*, ed. Shawqī Ḍayf (Cairo: Dār al-Maʿārif, 2nd edn, *c.* 1980/1401), p. 45.

4 *Bayān*, 17:294.

5 *Muw.* 2:255; *Muw. al-Zuhrī*, 2:171; *Muw. Suwayd*, p. 599.

Bibliography

The following is a list of the books referred to in the text, including the abbreviations used for the same. The Arabic definite article 'al-' is ignored for listing purposes.

al-Abshīhī, *al-Mustaṭraf*, al-Manṣūra: Dār al-Ghad al-Jadīd, 1430/2009.

al-Aghānī = al-Iṣfahānī, Abū l-Faraj, *Kitāb al-Aghānī*, ed. ʿAbd al-Amīr ʿAlī Muhannā and Samīr Jābir, 25 vols, Beirut: Dār al-Fikr, 1407/1986.

Aḥmad ibn Ḥanbal, *al-Musnad*, 12 vols, 2nd edn, Beirut: Dār al-Fikr, 1414/1994.

al-Bājī, *al-Muntaqā, Sharḥ Muwaṭṭaʾ al-Imām Mālik*, 7 vols, Beirut: Dār al-Kitāb al-ʿArabī, n.d. (originally Cairo: Maṭbaʿat al-Saʿāda, 1331–2/1913–14).

Bayān = Ibn Rushd, *al-Bayān wa-l-taḥṣīl wa-l-sharḥ wa-l-tawjīh wa-l-taʿlīl fī masāʾil al-Mustakhraja*, ed. Muḥammad Ḥajjī, 20 vols, Beirut: Dār al-Gharb al-Islāmī, 1404–7/1984–7.

Berg, Herbert, *The Development of Exegesis in Early Islam: The Debate over the Authenticity of Muslim Literature from the Formative Period*, Richmond: Curzon Press, 2000.

Berg, Herbert (ed.), *Method and Theory in the Study of Islamic Origins*, Leiden: Brill, 2003.

Brockopp, Jonathan, Review of Dutton, *Origins of Islamic Law, Journal of Islamic Law and Society*, 7 (2000), pp. 398–400.

Brockopp, Jonathan, 'Competing Theories of Authority in Early Mālikī Texts', in Bernard G. Weiss (ed.), *Studies in Islamic Legal Theory*, Leiden: Brill, 2002, pp. 3–22.

Calder, Norman, *Studies in Early Muslim Jurisprudence*, Oxford: Clarendon Press, 1993.

al-Dhahabī, *Tadhkirat al-Ḥuffāẓ*, 4 vols in one, Hyderabad: Dāʾirat al-Maʿārif al-ʿUthmaniyya, 1377/1958.

al-Dihlawī, Shāh Walī Allāh, *Ḥujjat Allāh al-Bāligha*, ed. Muḥammad Sharīf Sukkar, 2 vols, Beirut: Dār Iḥyāʾ al-ʿUlūm, 1410/1990.

Dutton, Yasin, 'ʿ*Amal v. Ḥadīth* in Islamic Law: The Case of *Sadl al-yadayn* (Holding One's Hands by One's Sides) When Doing the Prayer', *Islamic Law and Society*, 3 (1996), pp. 13–40.

Dutton, Yasin, 'Islam and the Environment: A Framework for Enquiry', in Harfiyyah Abdel Haleem (ed.), *Islam and the Environment*, London: Ta-Ha, 1998, pp. 56–74.

Dutton, Yasin, 'Juridical Practice and Madinan *'Amal: Qaḍā'* in the *Muwaṭṭa'* of Mālik', *Journal of Islamic Studies*, 10, no. 1 (1999), pp. 1–21.

Dutton, Yasin, *The Origins of Islamic Law: The Qur'an, the* Muwaṭṭa' *and Madinan* 'Amal, Richmond: Curzon, 1999.

Dutton, Yasin, 'The Qur'ān as a Source of Law: The Case of *Zakāt* (Alms-Tax)', in Robert G. Hoyland and Philip F. Kennedy (eds), *Islamic Reflections Arabic Musings: Studies in Honour of Alan Jones*, Oxford: Gibb Memorial Trust, 2004, pp. 201–16.

Dutton, Yasin, *Original Islam: Mālik and the* Madhhab *of Madina*, London: Routledge, 2007 [contains a translation of al-Rā'ī's *Intiṣār*, q.v.].

Encyclopaedia of Islam, 1st edn, Leiden/London: E.J. Brill, 1913–38; 2nd edn, Leiden: E.J. Brill/Brill, 1960–2002.

El Shamsy, Ahmed, *The Canonization of Islamic Law*, Cambridge: Cambridge University Press, 2013.

El Shamsy, Ahmed, 'Al-Shāfi'ī's Recension of Mālik's *Muwaṭṭa'*', Islamic Law Blog. Available online: https://islamiclaw.blog/2019/12/06/muwaṭṭa'-roundtable-al-shafi'is-recension-of-maliks-muwaṭṭa' (accessed 23 February 2021).

al-Fasawī, *Kitāb al-Ma'rifa wa-l-Tārīkh*, ed. Akram Ḍiyā' al-'Umarī, 4 vols, al-Madīna al-Munawwara: Maktabat al-Dār, 1410/1990.

al-Ghabban, Ali, *Les deux routes syrienne et égyptienne de pèlerinage au nord-ouest de l'Arabie Saoudite*, Cairo: Institute français d'archéologie orientale, 2011.

Goldziher, Ignaz, *Muslim Studies*, translated from the German *Muhammedanische Studien* (Halle a. S.: Max Niemayer, 1889–90) by C. R. Barber and S. M. Stern, 2 vols, London: George Allen & Unwin, 1967–71.

Haddad, G. F., Review of Dutton, *Original Islam: Mālik and the* Madhhab *of Madina*, *Muslim World Book Review*, 27, no. 4 (summer 2007), pp. 30–36. Available online: https://www.academia.edu/43228191/Review_of_Yasin_Duttons_Original_Islam_Malik_and_the_Madhhab_of_Madina (accessed 23 February 2021).

Hallaq, Wael B., 'Was al-Shāfi'ī the Master Architect of Islamic Jurisprudence?', *International Journal of Middle East Studies*, 25 (1993), pp. 587–605.

Hallaq, Wael B., 'From Regional to Personal Schools of Law? A Reevalution', *Islamic Law and Society*, 8 (2001), pp. 1–26.

Hallaq, Wael B., *The Origins and Evolution of Islamic Law*, Cambridge: Cambridge University Press, 2005.

Ḥamdān, Nadhīr, *al-Muwaṭṭa'āt*, Damascus: Dār al-Qalam, 1412/1992.

Ibn Abī Ḥātim, *Kitāb al-Jarḥ wa-l-ta'dīl*, 9 vols, Hyderabad: Dā'irat al-Ma'ārif al-'Uthmāniyya, 1360/1941.

Ibn Baṭṭūṭa, *Riḥla*, Beirut: Dār Ṣādir, n.d.

Ibn Farḥūn, *al-Dībāj al-mudhhab*, ed. Maʿmūn ibn Muḥyī al-Dīn al-Jannān, Beirut: Dār al-Kutub al-ʿIlmiyya, 1417/1996.

Ibn Ḥamdūn, Muḥammad al-Ṭālib, *Ḥāshiya ʿalā sharḥ Mayyāra al-ṣughrā li-manẓūmat al-Murshid al-muʿīn li-ʿAbd al-Wāḥid ibn ʿĀshir*, 2 vols in one, Beirut: Dār al-Fikr, 1392/1972.

Ibn Ḥajar al-ʿAsqalānī, *Tahdhīb al-tahdhīb*, 12 vols in six, Hyderabad: Dāʾirat al-Maʿārif al-Niẓāmiyya, 1325–7/1907–9.

Ibn Jubayr, *Riḥla*, Beirut: Dār Ṣādir/Dār Bayrūt, 1384/1964.

Ibn Māyaʾbā al-Shinqīṭī, Muḥammad Ḥabīballāh, *Iḍāʾat al-ḥālik min alfāẓ dalīl al-sālik ilā Muwaṭṭaʾ al-Imām Mālik*, 2nd edn, Beirut: Dār al-Bashāʾir al-Islamiyya, 1415/1995.

Ibn Mujāhid, *Kitāb al-Sabʿa fī l-qirāʾāt*, ed. Shawqī Ḍayf, Cairo: Dār al-Maʿārif, 2nd edn, *c.* 1980/1401.

Ibn Qutayba, *Taʾwīl mukhtalif al-ḥadīth*, ed. Muḥammad Zuhrī al-Najjār, Beirut: Dār al-Jīl, 1393/1972.

Ibn Saʿd, *al-Ṭabaqāt al-kubrā*, ed. ʿAlī Muḥammad ʿUmar, 11 vols, Cairo: Maktabat al-Khānjī, 1421/2001.

Ibn Wahb, *al-Muwaṭṭaʾ*, ed. Hishām ibn Ismāʿīl al-Ṣīnī, Hofuf: Dār ibn al-Jawzī, 1420/1999.

ʿIllīsh, Muḥammad Aḥmad, *Fatḥ al-ʿalī al-mālik fī l-fatwā ʿalā madhhab al-Imām Mālik*, 2 vols, Beirut: Dār al-Fikr, 1392/1972.

Imbert, Frédéric, 'Califes, princes et compagnons dans les graffiti du debut de l'Islam', *Romano-Arabica* 15 (2015), pp. 59–78.

Intiṣār = Muḥammad al-Rāʿī, *Intiṣār al-faqīr al-sālik li-tarjīḥ madhhab al-imām al-kabīr Mālik*, ed. Muḥammad Abū l-Ajfān, Beirut: Dār al-Gharb al-Islāmī, 1981.

Isʿāf = al-Suyūṭī, *Isʿāf al-mubaṭṭaʾ bi-rijāl al-Muwaṭṭaʾ*, appended to *Muw.* (q.v.).

Jones, Alan, 'The Dotting of a Script and the Dating of an Era: The Strange Neglect of PERF 558', *Islamic Culture*, 52 (1998), pp. 95–101.

Khalīl, *Mukhtaṣar*, ed. Aḥmad Naṣr, Beirut: Dār al-Fikr, 1401/1981.

al-Kilābī, Ḥayāt, *al-Nuqūsh al-Islāmiyya fī ṭarīq al-ḥajj al-Shāmī shimāl gharb al-Mamlaka al-ʿArabiyya al-Saʿūdiyya, min al-qarn al-awwal ilā l-qarn al-khāmis al-Hijrī*, al-Riyadh: Maktabat al-Malik Fahd al-Waṭaniyya, 2009.

Lecker, Michael, 'Biographical Notes on Ibn Shihāb al-Zuhrī', *Journal of Semitic Studies*, 41 (1996), pp. 21–63, esp. pp. 22–41 [reprinted in Michael Lecker, *Jews and Arabs in Pre- and Early Islamic Arabia*, Section XVI, Aldershot: Ashgate Variorum, 1999].

Lindstedt, Ilkka, 'Writing, Reading, and Hearing in Early Muslim-era Arabic Graffiti', International Qur'anic Studies Association (2017). Available online: https://iqsaweb.wordpress.com/2017/01/02/writing-reading-and-hearing-in-early-muslim-era-arabic-graffiti/ (accessed 23 February 2021).

Lowry, Joseph, 'Does Shāfiʿī Have a Theory of "Four Sources" of Law?', in Bernard G. Weiss (ed.), *Studies in Islamic Legal Theory*, Leiden: Brill, 2002, pp. 23–50.

Mad. = al-Qāḍī ʿIyāḍ, *Tartīb al-madārik wa-taqrīb al-masālik li-maʿrifat aʿlām madhhab Mālik*, ed. Aḥmad Bakīr Maḥmūd, 5 vols in three, Beirut: Manshūrāt Dār Maktabat al-Ḥayāt, 1387/1967.

Mālik ibn Anas, *Al-Muwaṭṭaʾ, The Royal Moroccan Edition, The Recension of Yaḥyā ibn Yaḥyā al-Laythī*, ed. Mohammed Fadel and Connell Monette, Cambridge, MA: Harvard University Press, 2019.

Maʿrūf, Bashshār ʿAwwād, 'The Muwatta' of Malik ibn Anas: Variations Among its Recensions and their Rationale'. Lecture given at SOAS, London, 24 October 2019. Available online: http://www.iccuk.org/news2.php?section=news&page=news195 (accessed 25 February 2021).

Melchert, Christopher, *The Formation of the Sunni Schools of Law, 9th-10th Centuries C.E.*, Leiden: Brill, 1997.

Mud. = *al-Mudawwana al-kubrā* (opinions of Mālik, Ibn al-Qāsim and others, compiled by Saḥnūn), 16 vols in six, Beirut: Dār Ṣādir, n.d. (originally Cairo: Maṭbaʿat al-Saʿāda, 1323–4/1905–6).

al-Murabit, Shaykh Abdalqadir, *Root Islamic Education*, 2nd edn, London: Madinah Press, 1993.

Muw. = Mālik ibn Anas, *al-Muwaṭṭaʾ* (transmission of Yaḥyā ibn Yaḥyā al-Laythī), printed with al-Suyūṭī's *Tanwīr al-ḥawālik*, 2 vols, Cairo: Maṭbaʿat Muṣṭafā al-Bābī al-Ḥalabī wa-Awlāduh, 1349/1930.

Muw. Ibn Bukayr = (transmission of Ibn Bukayr) two folios of the Ẓāhiriyya manuscript, No. 3780, illustrated in Nadhīr Ḥamdān, *al-Muwaṭṭaʾāt*, Damascus: Dār al-Qalam, and Beirut: al-Dār al-Shāmiyya, 1412/1992, pp. 116–19.

Muw. Ibn al-Qāsim = Mālik ibn Anas, *al-Muwaṭṭaʾ* (transmission of Ibn al-Qāsim, with the *Talkhīṣ* of al-Qābisī), ed. Muḥammad ibn ʿAlawī ibn ʿAbbās al-Mālikī, Jeddah: Dār al-Shurūq, 1405/1985.

Muw. Ibn Ziyād = Mālik ibn Anas, *al-Muwaṭṭaʾ* (transmission of ʿAlī ibn Ziyād), ed. Muḥammad al-Shādhilī al-Nayfar, Beirut: Dār al-Gharb al-Islāmī, 1400/1980.

Muw. al-Qaʿnabī = Mālik ibn Anas, *al-Muwaṭṭaʾ*, in the transmission of ʿAbdallāh al-Qaʿnabī, ed. ʿAbd al-Ḥafīẓ Manṣūr, Kuwait: al-Shurūq, n.d..

Muw. Sh. = Mālik ibn Anas, *al-Muwaṭṭaʾ* (transmission of Muḥammad ibn al-Ḥasan al-Shaybānī), ed. ʿAbd al-Wahhāb ʿAbd al-Laṭīf, Beirut: Dār al-Qalam, 1382/1963.

Muw. Suwayd = Mālik ibn Anas, *al-Muwaṭṭaʾ* (transmission of Suwayd al-Ḥadathānī), al-Manāma: Idārat al-Awqāf al-Sunniyya, 1415/1994.
Muw. al-Zuhrī = Mālik ibn Anas, *al-Muwaṭṭaʾ* (transmission of Abū Muṣʿab al-Zuhrī), ed. Bashshār ʿAwwād Maʿrūf and Maḥmūd Muḥammad, 2nd edn, Beirut: Mu'assasat al-Risāla, 1413/1993.
al-Nawawī, *Tahdhīb al-asmāʾ*, two parts, Cairo: Idārat al-Ṭibāʿa al-Munīriyya, n.d.
Ould Bah, Mohamed El Mokhtar, *Madkhal ilā uṣūl al-fiqh al-Mālikī*, Rabat: Dār al-Amān, 2011.
Powers, David, *Studies in Qur'an and Ḥadīth: The Formation of the Islamic Law of Inheritance*, Berkeley: University of California Press, 1986.
al-Saʿīd, ʿAbdallāh ʿAbd al-ʿAzīz, Muḥammad Shafīq Khalīl al-Bīṭār, al-Saʿd Sulaymān al-Saʿīd and Aḥmad Muḥammad al-Dāmigh, *Nuqūsh Ḥismā: kitābāt min ṣadr al-Islām shamāl gharb al-Mamlaka*, Riyadh: al-Majalla al-ʿArabiyya, 2017.
Savant, Sarah, 'A Tale of 3 "Versions"', *KITAB website*, 10 September 2017. Available online: http://kitab-project.org/2017/09/10/a-tale-of-3-versions/ (accessed 23 February 2021).
Schacht, Joseph, *The Origins of Muhammadan Jurisprudence*, Oxford: Clarendon Press, 1950.
Schacht, Joseph, 'Deux éditions inconnues du *Muwaṭṭa*'', in *Studi Orientalistici in Onore di Giorgio Levi Della Vida*, vol. 2, Rome: Istituto per l'Oriente, 1956, pp. 477–92.
Schacht, Joseph, 'Mālik b. Anas', in *Encyclopaedia of Islam*, 2nd edn, vol. 6, Leiden: E.J. Brill, 1991, pp. 262–5.
Schacht, Joseph, 'On Some Manuscripts in Kairouan and Tunis', *Arabica*, 14 (1967), pp. 225–58.
Schacht, Joseph, 'On Some Manuscripts in the Libraries of Morocco', *Hespéris-Tamuda*, 9 (1968), pp. 5–55.
Schoeler, Gregor, in collaboration with and translated by Shawkat M. Toorawa, *The Genesis of Literature in Islam: From the Aural to the Read*, rev. edn, Edinburgh: Edinburgh University Press, 2009.
al-Shāfiʿī, Muḥammad ibn Idrīs, *Kitāb al-Umm*, 8 vols, Beirut: Dār al-Fikr, 1400/1980.
al-Shaybānī, Muḥammad ibn al-Ḥasan, *Kitāb al-Ḥujja ʿalā Ahl al-Madīna*, ed. Mahdī Ḥasan al-Kīlānī al-Qādirī, 4 vols, 3rd edn, Beirut: ʿĀlam al-Kutub, 1403/1983.
Sheibani, Maryam, Amir Toft and Ahmed El Shamsy, 'The Classical Period: Scripture, Origins, and Early Development', in Anver M. Emon and

Rumee Ahmed (eds), *The Oxford Handbook of Islamic Law*, Oxford: Oxford University Press, 2018.

Tam. = Ibn ʿAbd al-Barr, *al-Tamhīd li-mā fī l-Muwaṭṭaʾ min al-maʿānī wa-l-asānīd*, 24 vols, Mohammedia: Wizārat al-Awqāf wa-l-Shuʾūn al-Islāmiyya, 1397–1411/1977–91.

al-Tirmidhī, *Sunan* [= *al-Jāmiʿ al-ṣaḥīḥ*], 5 vols, Cairo: Maṭbaʿat Muṣṭafā al-Bābī al-Ḥalabī wa-Awlāduh, 1st edn, 1356/1937, 2nd edn, 1395/1975.

ʿUtbiyya = Muḥammad al-ʿUtbī al-Qurṭubī, *al-Mustakhraja min al-asmiʿa*, also known as *al-ʿUtbiyya*, contained in Ibn Rushd, *al-Bayān wa-l-taḥṣīl wa-l-sharḥ wa-l-tawjīh wa-l-taʿlīl fī masāʾil al-Mustakhraja*, ed. Muḥammad Ḥajjī, 20 vols, Beirut: Dār al-Gharb al-Islāmī, 1404–7/1984–7.

Wakīʿ, *Akhbār al-quḍāt*, ed. Saʿīd Muḥammad al-Laḥḥām, 4 vols in one, Beirut: ʿĀlam al-Kutub, n.d.

Wymann-Landgraf, Umar F. Abd-Allah, *Mālik and Medina: Islamic Legal Reasoning in the Formative Period*, Leiden: Brill, 2013.

Zur. = al-Zurqānī, *Sharḥ al-Muwaṭṭaʾ*, 4 vols, Cairo: Maktabat al-Kulliyyāt al-Azhariyya, 1399/1979.

Index

This index does not include the separate terms Mālik, Medina, Messenger of Allah, or *Muwaṭṭaʾ*. The Arabic definite article 'al-' is ignored for listing purposes.

Abān ibn ʿUthmān [ibn ʿAffān] 19, 22–3, 101
ʿAbd al-ʿAzīz ibn Abī Salama al-Mājishūn 17, 72, 99
ʿAbd al-Raḥmān ibn ʿAwf 20, 23, 42, 96
ʿAbd al-Raḥmān ibn Ḥarmala al-Aslamī, Abū Ḥarmala 3, 34–5, 54, 56–7
ʿAbd al-Raḥmān ibn Mahdī 40, 45, 72
ʿAbd al-Raḥmān ibn al-Qāsim (shaykh of Mālik) 16, 31–2, 114
[ʿAbd al-Raḥmān] ibn al-Qāsim (student of Mālik), *see* Ibn al-Qāsim, ʿAbd al-Raḥmān
ʿAbdallāh ibn Abī Bakr [ibn Muḥammad ibn ʿAmr] ibn Ḥazm 16, 28, 71
ʿAbdallāh ibn ʿAbd al-Raḥmān ibn Maʿmar, Abū Ṭuwāla 34
ʿAbdallāh ibn Dīnār 16, 29, 53, 55
ʿAbdallāh ibn ʿUmar 20–2, 23–5, 29, 31, 36, 48, 50, 53–7, 73–4, 80–3, 100–1
ʿAbdallāh ibn Wahb 44, 71, 90, 97, 111, 128 n.23, 128 n.25, 128 n.26
ʿAbdallāh ibn Yazīd ibn Hurmuz 36–7
ʿAbdallāh ibn Yūsuf al-Tinnīsī 43–4
Abū Bakr (first caliph) 8, 20–1, 23–4, 26–7, 29, 31–2, 48, 90, 98–9
Abū Bakr ibn ʿAbd al-Raḥmān [ibn al-Ḥārith ibn Hishām] 16, 19, 22–3, 30, 73, 101
Abū Bakr ibn al-ʿArabī, Qadi 40
Abū Bakr [ibn Muḥammad ibn ʿAmr] ibn Ḥazm 17, 28, 34, 111
Abū Dāwūd 43–5
Abū Ḥanīfa 9, 42, 47, 50–1, 53, 56–8, 66, 77–8, 82, 86–7, 93, 95, 101, 129 n.51, 130 n.70
Abū Ḥātim 45
Abū Ḥudhāfa al-Sahmī 43
Abū Jaʿfar al-Manṣūr 25, 30
Abū Jaʿfar Yazīd ibn al-Qaʿqāʿ 36
Abū Muṣʿab al-Zuhrī, *see* al-Zuhrī, Abū Muṣʿab
Abū Salama ibn ʿAbd al-Raḥmān [ibn ʿAwf] 19–21, 23, 25, 27, 29, 35, 42, 84–5, 101
Abū Ṣāliḥ al-Sammān 29–31
Abū Yūsuf 42, 66, 77, 95
Abū l-Zinād ibn Dhakwān 16, 19, 26–7, 88, 90–1
Aḥmad [ibn Ḥanbal] 9, 39, 45, 67, 101
ʿĀʾisha 20–1, 24–6, 31, 54, 114–15
al-ʿAlāʾ ibn ʿAbd al-Raḥmān 16, 31–2
ʿAlī ibn Abī Ṭālib (fourth caliph) 23, 32, 73, 81, 100, 110
ʿAlī ibn al-Ḥusayn 23, 33
ʿAlī ibn Ziyād 41, 44, 59, 64, 90
ʿamal (of the People of Medina) 1, 5–6, 8, 37, 60–1, 63–79, 94, 96, 106, 108, 113–18
ʿAmra bint ʿAbd al-Raḥmān 25, 28
analogy 67–8
Asmāʾ 20, 26, 114
al-Awzāʿī 18, 40

Berg, Herbert 3
Brockopp, Jonathan 5–7
al-Bukhārī 40, 44, 69, 117

Calder, Norman 2, 5
consensus (*ijmāʿ*) 67–70, 113

'dead' land, development of 92–6

El Shamsy, Ahmed 3, 4, 45, 123 n.9, 130 n.69

fasting (Ramadan)
  making the intention before dawn 54

pre-dawn meal 55
sighting the new moon 53

gharar (uncertainty) 7–8, 65
Goldziher, Ignaz 2, 36, 108–11

ḥadīth 1–3, 40, 69, 77, 79
authenticity 40, 71, 113
collection of 18, 111
fabrication of 3, 109, 112–13
ḥadīth as 'knowledge' 18, 28, 65
Mālik's excellence in 39–40, 117
memorising or writing? 18, 28, 70
'people of' 70, 79
Prophetic / Companion / Successor 15, 59, 63, 69
unity of community around 105
ḥajj, being prevented from doing 73–4
Hallaq, Wael 123 n.8, 130 n.13
Ḥanafīs / Ḥanafī *madhhab* 1, 9, 42, 67, 73–4, 79, 107
Ḥanbalīs / Ḥanbalī *madhhab* 1, 9, 67
Hishām ibn ʿAbd al-Malik 17–18, 26, 35–6, 111
Hishām ibn ʿUrwa 16, 25–6, 92, 94, 101

Ibāḍīs 107
Ibn ʿAbd al-Barr 15, 19–20, 23, 30, 32–3, 35, 43
Ibn Baṭṭūṭa 107
Ibn Bukayr, *see* Yaḥyā ibn Bukayr
Ibn Jubayr 12
Ibn Hurmuz, *see* ʿAbdallāh ibn Yazīd ibn Hurmuz
Ibn Mahdī, ʿAbd al-Raḥmān 40, 45, 72
Ibn al-Madīnī 45
Ibn Mājah 44–5
Ibn al-Mājishūn, *see* ʿAbd al-ʿAzīz ibn Abī Salama al-Mājishūn
Ibn al-Qāsim, ʿAbd al-Raḥmān 41, 43–4, 59, 71, 75–6, 89, 91, 93, 111, 114, 128 n.23, 128 n.25, 128 n.26
Ibn Qutayba 113, 116
Ibn Shihāb [al-Zuhrī] 16–26, 28, 36, 47–8, 54–6, 73, 80–1, 84–6, 90–2, 94–5, 99, 111, 113, 125 n.8
Ibn Sīrīn, *see* Muḥammad ibn Sīrīn
Ibn ʿUmar, *see* ʿAbdallāh ibn ʿUmar
Ibn ʿUyayna, *see* Sufyān ibn ʿUyayna
Ibn Wahb, *see* ʿAbdallāh ibn Wahb
Ibn Ziyād, *see* ʿAlī ibn Ziyād
Isḥāq ibn ʿAbdallāh ibn Abī Ṭalḥa 29
ʿIyāḍ, Qadi 7, 70–1, 77, 79, 106

Jaʿfar ibn Muḥammad [ibn ʿAlī ibn al-Ḥusayn] 32–3
Jones, Alan 3
Jurists, Seven (or Ten) of Medina 19, 22–3, 25, 28–32, 35, 42, 73

Khārija ibn Zayd [ibn Thābit] 19, 22–3, 27, 35

al-Layth ibn Saʿd 65, 97–105, 108
Lowry, Joseph 130 n.13

Madhhab 4, 9–10, 60, 70, 79
Four *Madhhabs* 9, 39–40, 67, 106–7
Madārik 7, 70–2, 79, 106
Mālik ibn Abī ʿĀmir 11, 33
Mālikīs / Mālikī *madhhab* 1, 9–10, 61, 63, 67–8, 75–6, 79, 105, 107
Maʿn ibn ʿĪsā 44–5
Marwān 5, 73
Melchert, Christopher 2
Muʿāwiya [ibn Abī Sufyān] 21, 35, 48, 50, 73
Mudawwana 36–7, 44, 75–6, 89, 93, 110, 114
Muḥammad ibn Abī Bakr [ibn Muḥammad] ibn ʿAmr ibn Ḥazm 28, 71
Muḥammad ibn al-Ḥanafiyya 23
Muḥammad ibn al-Munkadir [ibn al-Ḥuḍayr] 33–4.
Muḥammad ibn Sīrīn 21
Mughalṭāy, al-Ḥāfiẓ 40
al-Murabit, Shaykh Abdalqadir 131 n.16
Muslim (*ḥadīth* transmitter) 40, 44, 117
Muṭarrif 43

Nāfiʿ (the *mawlā* of Ibn ʿUmar) 12, 16, 24–5, 29, 37, 125 n.9
Nāfiʿ (Qur'an reciter) 13, 125 n.9
Nāfiʿ ibn Mālik, Abū Suhayl 11, 33
al-Nasāʾī 44–5

oath of abstention from marital intercourse 72–3, 105

Powers, David 2
prayer
  how to hold one's hands 74–7, 107–8
  joining because of rain 100–1
  passing in front of someone 80–3

Qabīṣa ibn Dhu'ayb 19, 22–3
al-Qa'nabī 41, 43–5, 52, 56–9, 110–11
al-Qāsim ibn Muḥammad [ibn Abī Bakr] 8, 19, 21, 23–5, 28, 30–2, 48, 118
Qur'an
  2:196 74
  2:266–7 72
  2:278–9 7
  2:279 5
  2:282 102
  5:3 69
  6:145 67
  9:60 5
  9:100 98
  9:105 116
  16:8 90
Qutayba ibn Sa'īd 45

Rabī'a [ibn 'Abd al-Raḥmān] 12, 16, 25–6, 30, 37, 72, 84–5, 90–1, 99, 106, 116
Rajā' ibn Ḥaywa 21

Sa'd ibn Abī Waqqāṣ 64, 81, 83–4, 100
al-Saffāḥ, Abū l-'Abbās 25, 34
Saḥnūn 89–90, 93, 114
al-Saffāḥ, Abū l-'Abbās 25, 34
Sa'īd ibn al-Musayyab 17, 19–23, 25, 27, 39, 54, 73, 84–5, 99, 101
Sa'īd ibn Sulaymān ibn Zayd ibn Thābit 22, 35
Sālim ibn 'Abdallāh [ibn 'Umar] 17, 19–21, 23, 25, 39, 55–6, 81–2, 92
Sālim, Abū l-Naḍr 16, 29
Savant, Sarah 130 n.70
Schacht, Joseph 1–3, 108–9, 111–12, 115
Seven / Ten Jurists (of Medina) 19, 22–3, 25, 28–32, 35, 42, 73
al-Shāfi'ī 2–4, 9, 40, 45, 59, 66, 68, 78–9, 91–6, 101, 108, 117, 130 n.69, 130 n.13
Shāfi'īs 1, 9, 67, 79
Shāh Walī Allāh al-Dihlawī 40
Shamsy, Ahmed El *see* El Shamsy, Ahmed
al-Shaybānī 41–2, 45, 47, 50–4, 56–9, 66, 81–9, 93, 100, 108, 110–11, 130 n.70
Shī'a 1, 32, 107
Six Books (of *ḥadīth*) 43–5, 59, 69
Sufyān ibn 'Uyayna 39, 97
Suhayl ibn Abī Ṣāliḥ al-Sammān 16, 30–1
Sulaymān ibn 'Abd al-Malik 10, 34
Sulaymān ibn Yasār 19, 21–5, 27, 29, 30, 39, 47
Sumayy, the *mawlā* of Abū Bakr ibn 'Abd al-Raḥmān 16, 30
sunna 1–3, 6–8, 40, 48, 50, 60, 67–9, 70–2, 77, 79, 83, 91, 94–6, 98
Suwayd al-Ḥadathānī 41, 43, 45–7, 50, 52, 56–9, 110–11

testimony of one witness 101–3
al-Thawrī 40
al-Tirmidhī 9, 40, 44–5

'Ubaydallāh ibn 'Abdallāh [ibn 'Utba ibn Mas'ūd] 17, 19–20, 23, 29
'Umar ibn 'Abd al-'Azīz 22, 26, 28, 34, 46–7, 102–3, 111
'Umar [ibn al-Khaṭṭāb] (second caliph) 3, 20–1, 23–4, 27–8, 52, 54–5, 64, 71, 85, 88–90, 92, 94–6, 98–9, 101–4, 115–16
'Urwa ibn Udhayna 36–7, 110
'Urwa ibn al-Zubayr 3, 17, 19–20, 23, 25, 52, 101
usury 5, 7, 68
'Uthmān [ibn 'Affān] (third caliph) 11, 13, 22–3, 26, 32–3, 48, 53–6, 98–9, 102

al-Walīd ibn 'Abd al-Malik 22
al-Walīd ibn Yazīd ibn 'Abd al-Malik 25
water that dogs have licked 87–92
Wymann-Landgraf, Umar Abd-Allah, 4

Yaḥyā ibn Bukayr 41, 43, 45–6, 50, 55, 57, 59, 110–11
Yaḥyā ibn Sa'īd al-Anṣārī 16, 25, 99
Yaḥyā ibn Yaḥyā al-Laythī 41, 43, 45, 55–8, 63, 110–11, 130 n.69
Yaḥyā ibn Yaḥyā al-Tamīmī 44

zakāt 5, 56–8, 64
  of associates 104

buried treasure 84–7
collection 17–18
joint owners 103
mines 84–7
'Umar's document 17, 103
what *zakāt* is due on 46–53
Zayd ibn Aslam 16, 27, 80, 82, 90
Zayd ibn Thābit 5, 22–3, 35
al-Zuhrī, Abū Muṣ'ab 6–7, 41–2, 45–7, 50–2, 55–9, 110–11, 130 n.69

www.ingramcontent.com/pod-product-compliance
Lightning Source LLC
Chambersburg PA
CBHW061843300426
44115CB00013B/2485